WHAT THE BIBLE TEACHES ABOUT
THE END OF THE WORLD

This series of books sets out to present what the Bible actually teaches. We have in mind a readership made up of people of all ages who are comparatively new to the Christian faith or who are feeling their way towards it.

Inevitably, some of the topics considered may be easier to deal with than others. All those who have contributed to the series have in some way or other been involved in a teaching ministry, but in presenting this series of books we are not writing primarily for theological students. Our concern is to help people who are enquiring about the Christian faith and those who have come to believe but who have not had a Christian background. In recent years there has been a tendency to regard Christian doctrine lightly, and to emphasize Christian experience and Christian living. What is needed is a balance between the various aspects of the Christian faith, so that both our experience and our way of life may be measured against the yardstick of what the Bible teaches.

We therefore present this series in the prayerful hope that some seekers after truth may come through to a living faith, and that those whose experience of Christ is new may be built up to become mature men and women of God.

While each book stands on its own feet, we recommend that those who desire to gain a full-orbed picture of what Christianity is all about should study the series as a whole.

EDITOR

WHAT THE BIBLE TEACHES ABOUT

THE END
OF THE
WORLD
Bruce Milne

SERIES EDITOR: G. W. KIRBY

Tyndale House Publishers, Inc. Wheaton, Illinois

Unless otherwise stated, Bible quotations are from the Revised Standard Version
of the Bible.

Library of Congress Catalog Card Number 80-80181. ISBN 0-8423-7888-X,
paper. Copyright © 1979 by Bruce A. Milne. First published in Great Britain,
under the title *I Want to Know What the Bible Says about the End of the World*, by
Kingsway Publications, Ltd. Tyndale House edition published by arrangement
with Kingsway Publications, Ltd. All rights reserved. First Tyndale House print-
ing, July 1980. Printed in the United States of America.

CONTENTS

INTRODUCTION

The doorbell rang. A young man in a smart blue suit greeted me with a pleasant smile. 'Good evening,' he said, 'may I speak to you for a moment about the signs of the times and the end of the world?' Who hasn't had a similar experience? And who among us has not felt the attraction and fascination of such subjects? What does the future hold for mankind? Will man survive his present crisis and enter the twenty-first century? And in personal terms – what will the future hold for me? What about death and what lies beyond it?

All around us today we are witnessing a tremendous interest in, almost an obsession with, the future. Almost every news-paper and magazine carries its horoscope column, and astrologers are besieged by clients wanting their future destiny revealed to them. Science fiction has become a boom industry and the popularity of films dealing with the future appears to be increasing rather than diminishing.

The Christian world also reflects this cultural trend. Racily written paperbacks claiming to recount the biblical teaching on the events leading up to the end of the world have claimed sales reaching over a million copies.

Some Christians of course dismiss all this as so much immature dreaming – a sort of escapism from the pressures and challenges of the modern world. There is no doubt a measure of truth in that reaction, but it is not the whole truth. Man needs hope and he cannot really live without *some* vision of his future, a contention which the Bible supports. Gone is the day when we could dismiss the Bible's teaching about the future and the end of the world as so much myth and make-believe. Scholars in our century have been forced to recognize that the Bible's teaching about the Last Things belongs to the very heart and essence of its message.

The theme of this book is therefore right at the centre both of current questions and biblical faith. One of the tragedies, however, about so much present writing and speculation about the future is that it contains a great deal that is utterly fanciful and misleading. There is urgent need to listen again to God's word and allow all our thinking and dreaming about the future to be corrected and informed by his infallible truth. What follows is one attempt to do just that – to discover what the Bible teaches about the Last Things.

The doctrine of the Last Things has unfortunately, but perhaps not surprisingly, been an area of biblical truth which has often caused controversy and division. In expounding the Bible's teaching it is impossible to avoid touching on some of these areas of contention. I have attempted to handle these issues as simply and clearly as possible. You are warned, however, that chapters 3 to 6 where these issues are dealt with, may be less easily understood than the other chapters, particularly if this is your first opportunity to study this particular area of Christian doctrine.

1

THE KINGDOM OF GOD

The first question to be faced is – where do we begin our study of the Last Things? One answer might be – with the book of Revelation and its prophecies. We will certainly need to examine the book of Revelation at some point, but even a cursory glance at it shows that it uses many ideas which appear earlier in the Bible (e.g. the Lamb, Satan, angels, churches, thrones), and so we obviously need to start further back.

Another answer might be – with the teaching of Jesus about his return in passages like Mark 13. Certainly that is a very important passage indeed, but it will not quite do as our starting point. The reason is similar to the reason for not beginning with Revelation. Jesus, though he was the eternal Son of God, was in his incarnate life a Jew of the first century. He grew up within a Jewish home and community and he worshipped and ministered within the life of first-century Jewish religion. In particular Jesus shared with his contemporaries a recognition of the authority of the Old Testament Scriptures. He was taught them from childhood and his own teaching and ministry were clearly profoundly affected by his meditation upon them and his submission to their authority.

Jesus' teaching therefore cannot be fully grasped unless we set him in the world of the Old Testament and the under-standing of the Old Testament which prevailed among the Jews in the first century. This principle is as valid for interpreting what he has to say about the Last Things and the future as it is for interpreting anything else he taught. We can illustrate this from the Mark 13 section. Jesus commences his discourse by

referring to people who would come 'in my name' claiming
'I am he' (verse 6). This alludes to Jesus' claim to be the
Messiah. In verse 8 he speaks of his coming being associated
with 'the sufferings'. In verse 14 he refers to the 'desolating
sacrilege' being 'set up where it ought not to be'. Now none
of these allusions can be truly understood unless set within the
context of first century Jewish religion and the Old Testament
Scriptures upon which it was based.

Even now, however, we have to exercise care. The Old
Testament contains numerous sections which predict events in
the future, particularly in its last part known as 'the Prophets'
(from Isaiah to Malachi). Are these books the place where we
should begin our investigation? While there is no doubt that
these writings are highly relevant to a study of the Last Things
they in turn cannot be understood apart from the whole history
of God's relationship through Israel over the centuries. Thus,
for example, the terrible judgements uttered by the prophets on
Israel cannot be appreciated unless we are aware of what Israel's
obligations to God amounted to. The relationship between God
and Israel, however, arose out of certain fundamental aspects of
God's character and his purposes for the world, which are set
out at the beginning of the Bible in Genesis and Exodus.

Thus we arrive at the surprising but important conclusion
that the proper place to start our investigation of the *last* things
is with the *first* things, with who God is, and with his great
deeds of creation and redemption in the Old Testament.

God is the King

We begin at the beginning, then, and ask, who is God? What
is his relationship to the world and to man within it? We can
answer these questions in one statement – God is the King. He
is the Lord who rules over everything; he is God alone. Nothing
is more basic to the Old Testament than that conviction.

This kingship of God is shown in all of his works. It is shown
in a unique manner in creation. He made all things out of nothing
by his word (Genesis 1:1; Hebrews 11:3; Psalm 33:6; John 1:3;

Hebrews 1:2). Freely, by his almighty power, unaided by any other factor, he called all things into existence out of non-existence (Romans 4:17). Not only has God created all things but he upholds them continually by his word (Psalms 33:6; 104; 135:6–7; Nehemiah 9:6; Hebrews 1:3; Colossians 1:17). The great forces of the universe are all his servants and he is Lord over them all (Isaiah 40:12–31). God is also sovereign in his purposes in history. He works through all the events in the lives of men and nations to fulfil his own designs. If he so pleases he can as easily use pagan rulers and armies as those who claim allegiance to him (Isaiah 45:1–2; Psalm 22:28–29; Daniel 4:34–35). He is Lord and King over all.

The King is opposed

God is the King; but that is not the whole story as far as the Old Testament is concerned. God has an enemy who resists his rule. The Bible does not tell us much about where the devil came from or how he came to be in the first place. It is concerned with the thing that really matters as far as we are concerned – that God's enemy exists and that he is in the world. What is more, the devil has succeeded in enticing man on to his side with the result that this world is in a state of rebellion against its King.

Genesis 3 relates how it all started. In spite of God's love and provision for them Adam and Eve succumbed to Satan's temptation and disobeyed God, and through their sin the rebellion spread to the whole human race (Romans 5:12–13). The Old Testament documents the course of this revolt as it passes through the generations. Eventually it reaches down to our own time and involves us all.

Jesus taught this truth about the world in one of his parables (Mark 12:1–11). A man plants a vineyard, puts it into perfect working order and then lets it out to some tenants while he is away in another country. Eventually he sends a servant back home for some of the fruit, but the servant is beaten and sent back empty-handed. The same treatment is meted out to successive messengers until at last the owner sends his son and heir. The son is killed by the tenants. The application is clear: God is the owner; the vineyard is this planet which he has created for man. The tenants are first of all the Jews, God's chosen people who have been given a special enjoyment of God's goodness and blessing. Instead of thanking God and submitting gladly to him they rebel and climax their opposition by slaying his Son, their promised Messiah. In all this the Jews act as representatives of the whole human race. This parable is the story of our world.

God has not abdicated
This sorry picture is not the whole story, however. The first truth which we expounded remains in force; God is the King and he continues his reign. There may have been a revolt in God's kingdom; the vineyard, to use Jesus' picture, may have in some respects fallen into the hands of the tenants, but God is still the King and he is not indifferent to what is going on. The rebellion has not dethroned him or placed his rule in question even for a single instant. Indeed it is just at this point, in his reaction to man's folly and rebellion, that God shows that he *is* truly the King.

God's sovereign love

God loves man, that is why he made him. In his love he has committed himself to man. He has plans and purposes for our rebel race, and because he is God these plans cannot be finally thwarted. When we turn away from God he does not give us up but comes again to us. The creator becomes the redeemer.

The whole Old Testament is the story of how God has worked out his purposes. He was not taken by surprise when Adam and Eve sinned. He was of course grieved by it, as he is by all our sinning, but he was not overthrown. At the very moment of the fall God is found speaking to Adam and Eve of his plan to restore man to the place of greatness and to the relationship of fellowship with himself which had existed in Eden before their disobedience (Genesis 3:15). In fulfilment of this promise

God called Abraham and made a covenant with him, promising him an inheritance in the land of Caanan and assuring him that through the outworking of this covenant the whole human race would be blessed (Genesis 12:1–2; Hebrews 11:8–9). God renewed this covenant with Abraham's posterity from whom eventually the people of Israel sprang.

In his kingly love God chose Israel and made a covenant with them at Mount Sinai, after delivering them from Egypt by his power (Exodus 11–19; Deuteronomy 7:6ff.). Israel was given a special knowledge of God and his will. They were taught who he was and how he was to be approached and worshipped. God acted again and again on their behalf, delivering them from enemies of all kinds (cf. Psalm 78). He sent them prophets, teachers, great leaders and kings, and he gave them his word. (Deuteronomy 29:29).

Thus God remains King in spite of the opposition to his rule. He acts in sovereign mercy to bring a people into relationship with him. Yet even this redemptive purpose of God appears on the surface to be frustrated in the Old Testament period. Such is the perversity of Israel that she fails again and again to fulfil the terms of God's will for her. In spite of his blessing, his revelation, his interventions and deliverances, his leaders, kings and spokesmen, and in spite of the clarity and power of his word to them, they still rebel. But the rebellion is never total. There is always a remnant who remain loyal to God and who obey his will. The general achievement of Israel, however, is disappointing. She knows better than all the other nations what she ought to do. She has God's word and all the heritage of faith behind her. God has acted for her deliverance and salvation. Yet she does not truly obey him.

The hope of the kingdom

It is out of the pressures and tensions of this agonizing contradiction of God's rule that there arises in the Old Testament a longing for something more in the future, a yearning and a conviction that God will do something new which will vindicate his kingship beyond any question. This is the burden of the great prophets of Israel. True, they bring God's word to his people in the present. They denounce the evils they see around them and expose the apostasy of their people. They speak too of God's coming judgement upon Israel and the surrounding nations. But they have something else to say. They speak of a future hope, of a coming intervention of God in the affairs of Israel and indeed of the whole world. God's great acts of redemption in the past are evidence of his power and will to do something even greater in the future (Isaiah 24:23; 45:22–23; Zechariah 14:9–10; Zephaniah 3:15; Amos 5:18–19; Obadiah 15ff; Malachi 4:1ff).

So the Old Testament contains a third element in its unfolding story of God and his relationship to man, an element which is crucial for the theme of this book. First there is the fact that God is King. Second is the fact that God's rule is opposed. Third there is the conviction that the redeeming purpose of God in history operating through Israel is destined to attain a glorious future fulfilment, that the God who is now King is going to act on a coming day to overthrow all the rebellious forces and vindicate his rule over all the world.

The prophets speak of this coming time as 'the Day of the Lord' (Amos 5:18–19; Zechariah 14:1–2; Malachi 4:1–2). It will be associated with a particular figure, the Messiah. He will be God's personal instrument through whom the Day of the Lord will come in judgement for the nations and in deliverance for Israel. He will be a great ruler after the order of David (Isaiah 9:6–7; 11:1–2; Micah 5:2ff.; Daniel 7:13–14; Zechariah 6:12–13).

In the period after the close of the Old Testament this hope of the future act of God came to be expressed in a new idiom; it was spoken of as the 'new age' or 'the age to come'. As such it was contrasted with the 'old age' or 'this present age'. The distinction between 'this present age' and 'the age to come' appears in several writings which belong to the period between the Old and New Testaments (Enoch, 4 Ezra, Apocalypse of Baruch). By Jesus' day it was a familiar distinction, and it appears in the gospels at several points (cf. Matthew 12:32;

Mark 10:30). One further crucial development had taken place, however, by the time of Jesus' ministry: 'the age to come' was now being commonly spoken of as 'the kingdom of God' (cf. Mark 10:23–30; Luke 20:34–36; 18:29–30).

The kingdom has come

The significance of this development of ideas for our interpretation of the message of Jesus and indeed of the whole New Testament is immediately clear, for Jesus' central claim was that 'the kingdom of God has drawn near' (Mark 1:15; Matthew 12:28). Through his ministry and preaching it is now 'in the midst' (Luke 17:21; cf. Mark 2:19; Luke 11:20; Matthew 12:28; Luke 4:16–21; Matthew 11:2ff.; 13:16f.; Luke 18:28ff.; Mark 9:1; Matthew 16:28). The idea of the kingdom of God is the central category of Jesus' whole teaching, as these references show. Anyone who doubts this need only glance at a Bible concordance in order to be persuaded.

The ideas we have just discussed show us what Jesus meant by 'the kingdom of God'. It was not a geographical territory. It was not simply people doing God's will in a general moral sense, more or less the same as 'being good'. It was rather the quite specific thought that God's kingdom has now been established in his world with all its attendant judgement and blessing. 'The kingdom of God has come' is for Jesus another way of saying that the longed for day of salvation which the Old Testament had predicted centuries before has now arrived, that the new day of God's rule has dawned for the world, with all its shattering implications for human life and destiny.

The New Testament's terms

The idea of the kingdom of God does not appear as frequently in the later parts of the New Testament as it does in the gospels of Matthew, Mark and Luke. In Matthew it usually appears as the kingdom of heaven. This phrase is simply a synonym for the kingdom of God. Many Jews were so conscious of God's majesty and greatness that they did not feel it appropriate even to mention the sacred name of God, and instead used words which were especially associated with him. Thus they would use words like 'temple' or 'altar' or 'heaven' in place of the divine name. Kingdom of heaven therefore simply means kingdom of God. Jesus clearly used both titles, but Matthew has especially noted the kingdom of heaven usage which was particularly suited to his Jewish readership.

Another synonym for the kingdom of God was 'eternal life'. The Greek for eternal life literally means 'the life of the age [to come]'. This equivalent to the kingdom of God was also current among the Jews of Jesus' day, though its meaning has become a little obscured in the English translation 'eternal life'. The life of the age to come is of course eternal in duration, but the real point is its quality rather than its quantity; it is the 'life of the age to come', the life of the kingdom of God predicted in the Old Testament. John makes particular use of this idea in his exposition of the teaching of Jesus (John 3:16; 3:36; 4:14; 5:24; 10:28; cf. 1 John 5:11–12).

When the gospel began to spread into the non-Jewish world (what the Jews referred to as the Gentile world) the early Christian preachers naturally could not presuppose a knowledge of the Old Testament on the part of their congregations in the way they could when preaching to Jews. This meant that the idea of the kingdom of God, the life of the age to come, was not familiar to a Gentile audience. Indeed the whole notion of kingship was likely to be fundamentally misunderstood in the Gentile world. Jesus himself acknowledged the possibility of such a misunderstanding on one occasion when he contrasted the idea of greatness among his disciples with that among the Gentiles (Mark 10:42ff.). Among the Gentiles 'kingship' meant despotic rule as embodied in the kingship of Caesar in Rome. Thus when the message of the gospel began to spread widely into the Gentile world the early preachers tended to move away from speaking about the kingdom of God and to use other concepts which would be more meaningful and less open to misunderstanding. For example they tended to speak of 'salvation' which was a common idea in the Gentile world. They spoke of Christ's offer of salvation from sin and guilt and death, and the spiritual powers of evil (cf. Philippians 3:20–21; 2 Thessalonians 2:13–14; Romans 1:16–17; Acts 16:30–31). They also spoke of 'faith in Christ' which implied 'union with Christ' (cf. Romans 5:1; 8:1; Colossians 2:20; Ephesians 2:8ff.; Philippians 3:9ff.; etc.).

It is interesting to examine the Acts of the Apostles in this light. It is a sort of pivot-book between the gospels with their Jewish setting and the Gentile world of the later New Testament. In the Acts the category of the kingdom which predominates at the beginning (1:3, 6; 8:12; 14:22; 20:25; 28:23, 31) gradually gives place to 'believing' and having 'faith in Christ' (2:44; 4:32; 8:12; 8:37; 10:43; 16:31; 20:21, 25; 26:18). The replacement of the one by the other is only relatively complete, and that is as it ought to be, for these ideas are really equivalents (8:12; 20:25). Behind them all lies the Old Testament hope of the coming of a new age of God's rule among men. This was brought by Jesus. To believe in him was to be united with him and to share the life of the kingdom, the life of the age to come.

The kingdom is yet to come

What has all this to do with the future? A great deal. We can see the significance of this if we examine Jesus' teaching about the kingdom. We can divide his claims about the kingdom into two classes.

First: the kingdom of God *has come*. In his ministry and his proclamation of it the reign of God has drawn near and is now a reality in the midst of human history. As men and women trusted and followed him as his disciples they were entering this promised kingdom (Luke 11:20; Matthew 12:28; Luke 4:16–21; Matthew 11:2ff.; 13:16–17; Matthew 19:29; Luke 18:28ff.; Mark 9:1; Matthew 16:28; Luke 17:20–21).

Second: the kingdom *has still to come* in its fullness. Jesus of course anticipated that his coming death and resurrection would be absolutely critical for the establishment of God's kingdom. But the future dimension reaches out beyond that to his glorious future appearing (Matthew 6:10; 19:28; Luke

22:29–30; Mark 14:25; Matthew 13:24ff.; Mark 13; Matthew 24–25; Luke 21).

These two claims express the boundaries within which all Jesus' teaching on the kingdom of God – and hence all his teaching – needs to be understood. The kingdom has come, and yet it is still to come. Salvation has appeared and is now offered to all who believe, and yet it has still to be fully given and manifest. The powers of evil have been struck a mortal blow and yet their final overthrow is not yet.

Life between the ages

The tension between these two dimensions runs right through the New Testament. It is the context of the Christian life. On the one hand the new age has appeared and we have entered it by faith in the Lord Jesus Christ, the Messiah who has brought the promised kingdom into realization. On the other hand, however, the old age of sin and death and decay is still with us and will not be finally sloughed off until the end when the new age comes in its fullness. On the one hand salvation has come to us in Christ who is the Saviour; by his death and resurrection he has overcome the powers of sin and evil; guilt has been answered finally in his cross and by his sacrifice there. God's wrath has been for ever turned away from all who call on Christ to save them. And yet, on the other hand, the fullness of salvation awaits the future culmination of God's triumph. We are saved now eternally, and yet we are saved in hope. On the one hand the Christian is a new man who is united with Christ and has shared in Christ's death and resurrection and reign. He has arisen from the grave of sin and now lives in the power of the resurrection and shares the powers of the new age of the kingdom. But on the other hand the 'old man' is still a painful and persistent reality dragging the Christian below the moral attainments to which his new life directs him.

Thus there is a tension which runs right through the New Testament and through the experiences of the people of God. We rejoice in the coming of the kingdom, in the fact of eternal salvation, in the blessings of the new age in our union with

Christ; and yet we long for our full deliverance, the full coming of the kingdom, the completion of our salvation and the emergence of the new man in Christ in all the fullness of his powers.

The Holy Spirit and the future

This whole 'position' of the Christian and the church is reflected in the biblical teaching on the Holy Spirit. The Spirit is seen in the Old Testament as the person of the Godhead through whom in a special sense the powers of the kingdom of God are manifest among men and women. The age to come, the age of the kingdom, was to be pre-eminently an age of the Spirit (Ezekiel 36:26ff.; Joel 2:28–29; Jeremiah 31:31ff.; Isaiah 44:3–4; 11:2; 61:1–2). Thus when Jesus seeks to authenticate his claim for the coming of the kingdom through his ministry he appeals to the power of the Spirit manifest through him (Matthew 12:28; Luke 11:20). At Pentecost, when the Spirit is poured out upon the church and the people demand an explanation, Peter recalls the Old Testament promises of the coming of the Spirit. 'This is what was spoken by the prophet Joel' (Acts 2:16ff.; cf. Joel 2:28–29).

What was spoken of and promised by the prophet Joel? Quite simply, the kingdom of God, or in Joel's terminology, the 'Day of the Lord'. The Holy Spirit is the life of the kingdom of God, the life of the new age (Romans 14:17). Thus only as we are regenerated by the Spirit can we enter the kingdom of God, as Jesus has to point out to Nicodemus (John 3:3ff.). The reality of the Spirit in the life of God's people is therefore the essential mark of our being truly within God's kingdom and having received the life of the age to come. But all this is only provisional, and that is why the New Testament again and again speaks of the Holy Spirit in terms of his being a foretaste or first instalment of the life of glory (cf. Romans 5:4–5; 8:15–17; 23ff.; 2 Corinthians 1:22; 5:5; Ephesians 1:13–14; 4:30). He is the guarantee of our inheritance. He gives us the new life of the kingdom within the limits and measure of this present point in time when the kingdom has still to come in fullness and the old age of sin and decay has not yet been thrown off. He is the guarantee that we shall share in that coming glory when the life which we now enjoy through the Spirit will burst out into its fullness and we shall know the true blessedness of life in the kingdom, life under God's rule.

What it all means

We have sought to build up all this biblical teaching from its beginnings back in the earliest relationship of God and man at the dawn of time, right through the Old Testament experience of the people of God and on to the ministry of Jesus and the apostles. This brings us right up to Christian experience today, and then leads us to two fundamental points.

1. The Christian's hope for the future is not something different from, or in any way foreign to his whole faith and relationship with God. The Last Things are in fact simply the First Things come to full flower. The God we meet in this area of Christian truth is precisely the same God we meet in every other area. The Christian hope is all of a piece with the Christian's faith at every other point. The Bible's teaching about the Last Things is therefore an integral element within the whole of biblical religion. All of God's activity in the past and all of his purposes in the present are with a view to what he has sworn to do in the future.

The content of this book is therefore a natural and essential part of the entire range of biblical doctrine and no understanding of Christian truth can possibly neglect it. Indeed every single Christian doctrine – whether of God, or man and sin, or the person and work of Christ, or the Spirit, or the church and sacraments – finds its goal and point of focus in the doctrine of the Last Things. The truths which will occupy us in this book are integral to the whole sweep of biblical teaching and therefore are emphatically *not* a peculiar concern of those with a special interest in the future, or those weary of life in this world, or those who long to escape from the harsh realities of the present into a future world of make-believe. All these suggested origins of an interest in the Last Things need to be uncompromisingly resisted. For the Bible the Last Things are part of all the other things, and indeed none of the other things can be correctly understood unless the Last Things are brought into the picture. In examining the Last Things we are simply looking at the religion of the entire Bible as it bursts into fullest flower.

2. By its nature Christian faith looks to the future. All its native instincts direct it forward towards the coming day in which God's purposes are to be fulfilled. All our experience of God in the present points us to the coming day when God's work of grace in us and through us will come to completion. The Christian who has entered the kingdom and stands with all the people of God within the sphere of the Spirit and the powers of the age to come will inevitably long and yearn for the fullness of these realities at the end of the present age. Thus the Christian should feel no shame about a concern with the Last Things. He should rather feel a very real shame about neglecting them. It belongs to the very essence of the Christian faith to reach out into the future for all that God has yet to do in the climax of his purposes at the end of the age.

In these last paragraphs we have referred to the fulfilling of God's purposes, the fullness of the kingdom, and so on. But in the Bible the whole reality of the Christian hope is most commonly expressed in more personal terms ... as the return in glory of the Lord Jesus Christ. The two stages of the coming of the kingdom, that which has come and that which has still to come, correspond to the two stages of the ministry of Christ. He is the one who has come and who is to come. The two phases of the kingdom are the two advents of the King. As we move on now to expound the different facets of what the Bible teaches about the future, the place to start is clear ... the return of Christ, and to this we now turn.

2

THE RETURN OF THE LORD

The centrality of the Lord's return

The most important thing the Bible teaches about the Last Things is that Christ is coming again. This is what it's all about. This is what the future holds for the Christian – the coming of his Lord. Christian hope is in the end quite simply hope of *him*.

The first appearing of the Lord was the central point in history, the hinge of all history, the decisive moment from which we date all our time. Every page of the history books and indeed every copy of our daily newspaper bears testimony to the significance of Christ's first coming, because all human events are dated from his birth.

Christ's second coming will be similarly crucial, for by it he will finalize all history. His second coming will be the hinge which links human history in this world with the life of the world to come.

The New Testament in all its major passages dealing with the future and the Last Things reflects this concentration upon the Lord and his appearing. Jesus himself in his great exposition of the Last Things in Mark 13 (cf. Matthew 24–25; Luke 21:5–28) sees the climax in these terms – 'then they will see the Son of man coming in clouds with great power and glory' (Mark 13:26). Everything leads up to and prepares for that. The coming of the Lord is the central reality. Preaching soon after Pentecost the apostle Peter expressed the Christian hope thus – '[God will] send the Christ appointed for you, Jesus' (Acts 3:20; cf. 17:31). Paul summarizes the hope in writing to the Philippians in a similar way – 'we await [from heaven] a Saviour, the Lord Jesus Christ' (Philippians 3:20; cf. 1 Corinthians 15:23; 1 Thessalonians 4:15–16; 2 Thessalonians 1:7; 2:1). The other New Testament writers make exactly the same emphasis when they refer to the Christian hope (cf. Hebrews 9:28; James 5:7; 1 John 3:2). Appropriately the New Testament closes with a prayer for his coming: 'Come, Lord Jesus!' (Revelation 22:20) in response to his reassurance to us, 'Surely I am coming soon.'

The centring of the Christian hope on the personal return of the Lord Jesus Christ needs to be underlined. It is possible to become so involved in the intricacies of prophetic fulfilment or with a study of the accompanying events that we can miss the central event. Like the pussycat in the nursery rhyme which was distracted in the presence of its sovereign by the 'little mouse under her chair' it is possible to be distracted from the really important thing, or rather the really important person. The Christian hope for the future is not a timetable of events. It is not concerned finally with a series of impersonal happenings. Its heart is nothing other than the expectation of the personal appearing of the Lord. If we find that our interest in the Last Things is centred elsewhere than in the Lord himself, then we are already out of step with Scripture. In this area of biblical truth, as in all the others, the golden rule is – keep your eyes on Jesus. He is the centre of God's revelation; he is the centre of God's redemption; and he is the centre of the Christian hope. We need in this area also to make the prayer of the Greeks our own: 'we wish to see Jesus.' (John 12:21.)

He is not absent .

The commonest term used in the New Testament for the second advent is *parousia* (cf. Matthew 24:3, 27, 39; 1 Corinthians 15:23; 1 Thessalonians 2:19; 3:13; 4:15; 2 Thessalonians 2:1, 8; James 5:7ff.; 2 Peter 1:16; 3:4, 12; 1 John 2:28). This word means 'coming', 'arrival' or 'presence'. It was used in the first century for the visit of an emperor or other distinguished person.

It conveys the idea that the Lord's return will be a definite and decisive action on his part. There will not be anything vague or uncertain about it. The Lord will do something which will be visible to all and unmistakably *his* act. He will come himself, as surely as he came in the incarnation.

In using this biblical term however we need to guard against misunderstanding. The fact that Scripture speaks of the Lord as 'coming' to us at the end of the age does *not* mean that he is therefore absent at the moment. Any such implication of *parousia* is dismissed by the other two New Testament words used for the second advent. The first of these is *apokalupsis* (cf. 1 Corinthians 1:7; 2 Thessalonians 1:7; 1 Peter 1:7; 4:13; 1:13). This word means 'revelation'. The Lord's coming will reveal who he is and what the world really is. It will be a time for things which are now hidden to come to light and be disclosed. There is no hint here of any present absence of the Lord. Similarly with the other term *epiphaneia* (cf. 2 Thessalonians 2:8; 1 Timothy 6:14; 2 Timothy 4:1, 8; Titus 2:13). This means 'appearing' or 'manifestation'. It also clearly reflects the thought of making known and making visible things which are secret and invisible at present. It carries the idea of drawing back a veil so that what is there already may be truly seen for what it is. Neither of these latter words imply the Lord's absence in the present.

Quite apart from these terms, any notion of Jesus being 'absent' is dismissed by the way in which the New Testament speaks of salvation. The essence of salvation is believing and trusting in the Lord Jesus in such a way that our lives are really caught up in his. A believer in Christ is a person whose life is made one with the Lord. We live in him and he lives in us (cf. John 14:18–23; 15:1–5; Romans 6:1–4; Galatians 2:20; Ephesians 2:5–6; Colossians 2:12; 3:1–3; etc.). His promise, 'I am with you always,' is one of the most triumphant statements of the entire Bible, and also one of the most precious to believing hearts. Every time Christians gather for worship they are assured that 'there am I in the midst' (Matthew 18:20). An experience of the living presence of Jesus is the very heart of

Christianity. He is no absent friend for whose return we must wait in emptiness.

Another reason why we ought to dismiss any thought of the Lord's 'absence' in the present is that it implies that his first coming did not really achieve a decisive victory over sin and evil. Sin always separates from God (Isaiah 59:2; cf. Genesis 3:24). If we are still separated from the Lord after his work of redemption then everything has still to be done at his second coming, and it becomes difficult to see what kind of victory he has won. But to think like that is completely contradictory to the spirit of the New Testament, when it speaks of Jesus' death and resurrection (Romans 5:15–21; 8:14–16; 5:1–11; 8:31–39; 1 Corinthians 15:20; 54–56; Galatians 4:4–7; Ephesians 1:3–8; 2:4–6; Colossians 2:12; 1 Peter 1:1–9; 1 John 5:1–21). The work of Christ at his second advent is to carry through into fulfilment the victory which he won through his first. The two advents belong together. There is nothing which the second coming will bring which the first has not already brought in principle.

... But we still look for his coming
In refuting the idea that the Lord is 'absent' in the present we need to be careful not to over-balance on the other side and give the impression that everything has already been achieved and *nothing* remains to be done. That too is wrong. Although the early Christians rejoiced in the victory which the Lord Jesus had won for them over sin, death and hell, and although they exulted in his presence with them day by day, they still longed for the return of the Lord (cf. Matthew 9:15; John 7:34; 8:21–22). 'Come, Lord Jesus!' (Revelation 22:20) is the cry which echoes throughout the *whole* New Testament and not just in those parts written at times of trial and violent persecution, such as the book of Revelation. For example, Paul writes just as ardently of the Christian hope when writing to the Philippians and the Thessalonians, where persecution was a less significant feature and things were going forward well and there was much encouragement (Philippians 3:20; 1 Thessalonians 4:13ff.).

There have been periods in the history of the church when Christians have been in danger of forgetting this. They have claimed that the church is in fact God's kingdom on earth with all the authority and glory of the Lord. In effect they have made the return of the Lord superfluous because they claim already to have all the blessings of his reign here and now.

The truth lies in keeping these two aspects in balance. On the one hand we rejoice here and now in the victory of Christ over all his foes and his presence with us by faith. On the other hand we are aware of the many ways in which his victory is not realized in our lives and we long for the fuller relationship with him which awaits us at his coming. And so we cry in yearning anticipation: 'Come, Lord Jesus!'

It isn't dispensable

Attempts have been made from time to time to deny the truth of the *parousia* and to suggest that it is not a particularly important aspect of the Christian faith. The suggestion is that those who believe in it are a little unbalanced and over-enthusiastic in their outlook. Thinking people, so it is suggested, are not really able to accept this teaching with its frankly supernatural emphasis. But in fact, so the story goes on, we can dispense with it anyway without losing anything that is really essential to the Christian faith. Just how inaccurate this last statement is will be clear as we go on. It is a complete nonsense to suggest that nothing of importance is lost if we jettison the doctrine of the Lord's return. In fact it is impossible to retain a Christianity which is recognizably the religion of the Bible without it. Not that we are committed of course to some of the rather weird interpretations of events connected with the *parousia* which some writers have espoused. We will make that point clearly in the next chapter. But the central fact, the visible appearing of the Lord Jesus Christ as a decisive event at the culmination of human history, *that* is not dispensable. To deny that is to cut the cord which binds us to historical Christian faith.

In view of such denials however it is well to examine how

secure are the biblical foundations of this great truth. The teaching on the Lord's return is found in both Old and New Testaments.

The Old Testament evidence

The Old Testament passages which refer to the Lord's return are in general those which speak of the glories of his messianic kingdom in terms which have clearly not found fulfilment in his first coming. Such a passage is Isaiah 11:1–10. Here the Messiah is thought of as a king from the line of David, 'a shoot from the stump of Jesse, and a branch ... out of his roots' (verse 1), 'the root of Jesse' (verse 10). The New Testament writers later saw this as a direct reference to the Lord Jesus Christ (cf. Acts 13:23; Romans 15:12). The passage, however, speaks of the influence of his rule in terms of universal judgement: 'he shall smite the earth with the rod of his mouth, and with the breath of his lips he shall slay the wicked' (verse 4); universal peace: 'the wolf shall dwell with the lamb, and the leopard shall lie down with the kid ... they shall not hurt or destroy in all my holy mountain' (verses 6–9); and universal knowledge of God: 'the earth shall be full of the knowledge of the LORD as the waters cover the sea' (verse 9). Patently these things have not yet come to realization. Hence they most obviously refer to the fullness of the rule of the Messiah after his glorious return.

Of similar import is a psalm such as Psalm 2. Here the Messiah is referred to as the kingly Son of God: 'I have set my king on Zion .... You are my Son,' (verses 6–7). The New Testament is again in no doubt that this is a prefiguring of the Lord Jesus (cf. Acts 13:33; Hebrews 1:5; 5:5; Matthew 3:17; 2 Peter 1:17). But this Son according to the psalm is destined to inherit the whole earth: 'I will make the nations your heritage, and the ends of the earth your possession' (verse 8); and he is also to be the instrument for the judgement and overthrow of evil in the world: 'You shall break them with a rod of iron, and dash them in pieces like a potter's vessel' (verse 9). Again, while we certainly discern the fulfilment of these prophecies in principle in the historic ministry of Jesus and his continuing ministry through his church in every age, the *full* terms of this lie beyond the limits of history as we experience it. They point us unmistakably forward to the return of the Lord and all that that will involve for him and for the world. Other similar passages are: Genesis 3:15; Deuteronomy 18:18–19; 2 Samuel 7:16; Psalms 72; 45; 89:3–4; Isaiah 2:1–5; 9:6–7; 40:3–5; 49:6; 53:10–12; 61:2; Jeremiah 23:5–6; 33:15; Daniel 7:13–14; Micah 4:1–3; Zechariah 3:8–9; 6:12–13.

There is also in the Old Testament one very important passage which refers directly to the coming of the Lord in glory. In Daniel 7:13–14 the prophet sees visions in the night of the end of the ages – 'behold, with the clouds of heaven there came one like a son of man ... and to him was given dominion and glory and kingdom, that all peoples, nations and languages should serve him; his dominion is an everlasting dominion, which shall not pass away ....' This passage is one of the most important in the whole Bible as far as the Lord's return is concerned. Jesus himself quotes it in his discourse on the end of the age (Mark 13:26; cf. Matthew 24:30; Luke 21:27) and again at his trial (Mark 14:62; cf. Matthew 26:64; Luke 22:69), and there are clear echoes of it in Revelation 1:7, 13; 14:14; and 1 Thessalonians 4:17.

The New Testament evidence

It has been computed that there are over two hundred and fifty clear references to the return of the Lord in the New Testament. Obviously we cannot list them all here, but the most important ones will be referred to or else discussed at some length in the chapters which follow. Here are some of the principal New Testament passages which refer directly to the return of the Lord Jesus Christ – Matthew 24–25; Mark 13; Luke 21; John 14:3; Acts 1:11; 3:20; 17:31; 1 Corinthians 15:23ff.; Philippians 3:20–21; 1 Thessalonians 4:13–5:11; 2 Thessalonians 1:7ff.; Hebrews 9:28; James 5:7; 1 Peter 1:7; 2 Peter 3:8–13; 1 John

2:28; 3:2–3; Revelation 1:7–8; 22:20. The range of these references shows unambiguously that the teaching on the *parousia* of the Lord runs right across the New Testament writings. It is found in all the gospels, Acts, the letters of Paul, Peter, James and John, Hebrews and the book of Revelation.

The fact of the Lord's return

All this evidence should make it abundantly clear that in referring to the second coming of Christ we are not speaking of a doctrine which can be found only in some obscure passage of the Old Testament, or that in believing in the Lord's return we are dependent for our biblical authority on highly imaginative interpretations of symbolic visions. This thing lies open for all to see on the surface of the Bible and appears clearly and consistently throughout its pages and in all its principal sections.

It follows therefore that the person who denies this teaching is not just telling us something about his views on the Last Things, but is making quite clear also his rejection of the word of God. The references are too frequent, too unambiguous, too precise to be ignored. To reject this truth is to reject the authority of Scripture in any meaningful sense and to be thrown back upon the limited and precarious authority of one's own personal judgement and experience, or the highly unstable authority of 'modern thought' or 'the latest theological opinion'.

How thankful we may be that we are not left at the mercy of such uncertainties. We have God's own eternal word in which to rest our hopes, the word of God which cannot be broken (John 10:35). God has spoken – the Lord is coming! Hallelujah!

It is worth adding that the fact of the return of Christ derives from God's revelation in the Bible and not in the first instance from the events of history. Our conviction concerning Christ's appearing ought not to be tied to a particular reading of the international political scene or the deep sense of crisis of our age. We will explore this issue more fully in the next chapter but it is to the point to draw attention to it here. It is a plain fact of Christian history that Christians in a number of generations have become so persuaded that the political events of their day fitted so precisely into the biblical 'signs of the times' that the Lord was surely coming in their lifetime. Thus, in a subtle way, their conviction ceased to rest in the word and promise of God alone, but alongside that they were really resting upon another foundation, viz. their reading of the events of their times. The result of this was that when their Lord did not come and their reading of the times was shown to be mistaken, they often in reaction lost all their conviction concerning the Lord's return and were robbed of their Christian hope.

The story of history has been of an ebb and flow of optimism and pessimism. Today the pendulum has swung to pessimism. Indeed it has probably swung further in that direction than in any previous age. But that *in itself* does not necessitate the return of the Lord in our generation. The pendulum may swing back again. If it does, that will in no way invalidate the glorious fact of Christ's appearing, for it rests not in the ebb and flow of history, or on the fallibilities of our reading of history, but on something objective and unshakable – on the sure word and promise of God. That is where we need to rest our conviction concerning the fact of Christ's return.

The nature of the Lord's return

If anyone is looking to this author, or any other for that matter, to furnish them with an exhaustive, detailed description of the second coming of Christ, then he is doomed for disappointment. A full description simply cannot be given in the nature of the case.

Describing the indescribable

The *parousia* will be an event which is different in kind from the series of events which go to make up our human history. It will be the *final* event, the culmination of all history. It will be an event in which the glorious Lord who is beyond all our limited experience will manifest himself. The only events which are real parallels are the creation of the world out of nothing, the Lord's virgin conception and his resurrection from the dead. It is not accidental that the Bible does not attempt a detailed description of any of these. One should refer also to a number of passages in the Bible which speak of special manifestations of God to men and women. The technical name for these is theophanies (cf. Genesis 15:12–17; Exodus 3:1–6; 19:16–25; Joshua 5:13–15; 1 Kings 19:9–13; Ezekiel 1:1–28; Daniel 7:11–28; Matthew 17:1–8; Acts 9:1–9; Revelation 1:12–18). In these revelations something of God's transcendent majesty and glory was disclosed to men and women. The effect was always the same. The observers were completely overwhelmed (Genesis 15:12; Exodus 3:6; Joshua 5:14; 1 Kings 19:13; Ezekiel 1:28; Daniel 10:7–17; Matthew 17:6; 28:4; Acts 9:4; Revelation 1:17), and the reports they subsequently gave are clearly attempts to describe the indescribable.

The Lord's return will be a supreme instance of theophany, and so by the nature of the case a detailed description is not possible. A detailed description would in fact destroy the mystery of it, and so make it cease to be a unique act of God; it would simply become part of the run of 'normal' human history. All this does not mean that we can say *nothing* about theophanies. Nor is it to say that we cannot discern the very clear impact of these events upon human history. But we cannot give a full description of them, and indeed we shall never be in a position to do so. Similarly we cannot fully describe the Lord's return.

Nor is this simply a matter of a general biblical or theological principle. Jesus says exactly this himself when discussing with his disciples 'the sign of his coming and the close of the age' (Matthew 24:3). 'For as the lightning comes from the east and shines as far as the west, so will be the coming of the Son of man' (Matthew 24:27). Now to liken the event to a flash of lightning was to draw attention to its essentially mysterious character. For men of the first century like Jesus' disciples, lightning was an essentially mysterious phenomenon. It typified the strange power of God in and over his world. The *parousia* is an event of this order, mysterious and going beyond all our normal experience.

Beware of blueprints

It follows therefore that the man who claims to have a detailed blueprint of the events of the Lord's return is suspect from the very outset. To be able to wrap it all up is in fact to miss it altogether. Indeed, there is almost a sense in which the man who has it all worked out is not really our friend, because he is in danger of changing the Lord's return into something it is not. He is changing its character and making it something less than the divine act of which Scripture speaks, and robbing God of his glory in it.

It is because the return of the Lord is of this mysterious character that the Bible resorts to symbol and imagery to refer to it. We ought not therefore to react against the symbols even if we find many of them puzzling. Symbol is the price we need to pay to retain it as an act of *God*.

Having clarified this point we again need to balance it quickly. To assert that all we can say about the return of the Lord involves symbols does not mean we can say or know nothing about it. It is at this point that many modern writers go wrong. The symbols of Scripture are God-inspired, and not the product of an over-heated human imagination. They are as surely as any other words of Scripture 'God-breathed' (2 Timothy 3:16) and therefore infallible and worthy of our utter trust and reliance. God addresses us in language which by the nature of the case employs the symbolic. But in his condescension he has chosen exactly those symbols which will, if correctly interpreted, convey to us as much knowledge of the Lord's return and the accompanying events as we need to know. Thus our task is to accept the Bible's teaching on the *parousia*, including all the symbolic passages, just as we accept any other section of Scripture. We take it from his hand believing that as a good Father who loves us and desires our good he will not wilfully mislead us, and then seek as faithfully as we can to interpret the biblical teaching in the conviction that in this way we will arrive at such a knowledge of these things as is possible for us, even if at the end of it all we can only know 'in part' (1 Corinthians 13:12).

What it will be like
What then may we assert concerning the Lord's return?

1. It will be a *glorious* return. It will be a return in 'power and great glory' (Matthew 24:30–31; cf. Daniel 7:13–14). At his coming 'every eye will see him' (Revelation 1:7). It will be 'the appearing of the glory of our great God and Saviour Jesus Christ' (Titus 2:13; cf. 2 Thessalonians 1:9).

In this respect the second advent will stand in sharp contrast to the first. The Lord's first coming was an essentially obscure event. True, the angels poured out their praises in the heavens, but only for the wondering ears of a company of humble shepherds. True, the star shone in the heavens, but only a group of eastern seers were made aware of its significance. For the most part the coming of God into the world in the wonder of Christmas passed virtually unnoticed. Nor were the terms of it exactly calculated to capture the headlines, the smelly stable in Bethlehem, an animal trough for a cradle, a humble peasant home for his human environment, a ministry to and among the 'common people' of his society, and in the end an ignominious death as a convicted criminal. True, he attained a certain prominence in his own land and among his own people. But even that was limited. The Jewish historian of the period, Josephus, gives him no more than a paragraph. Even that reference is disputed, though many scholars today accept its authenticity. The Roman historians hardly mention him at all. And although two thousand years later there are millions in every part of the world who have come to know and trust him as God and Saviour, vast segments of the human family remain in ignorance of his coming, or, if they do hear of it, shrug it aside as of no consequence to the running of their lives.

At his return all that will change. It will be a public and glorious manifestation of his person. Gone for ever will be the weakness and the obscurity; now will be the glory, the kingship and the acclaim. All men and women from every age of history will be confronted by his person and forced to acknowledge his triumph, for every knee will bow and 'every tongue confess that Jesus Christ is Lord' (Philippians 2:10–11).

The glorious nature of his coming is expressed in the reference to the 'clouds of heaven' (Matthew 24:30; Daniel 7:13; cf. Mark 13:26; Luke 21:27; Acts 1:9, 11; Revelation 1:7). Clouds are particularly significant in the biblical history of salvation. In the Old Testament the cloud signified God's glory and presence among his people (Exodus 13:21–22; 24:15–18; 2 Chronicles 5:13–14; Isaiah 6:4; Ezekiel 1:4ff.; 44:4; 5:13–14) hence in the New Testament the appearance of clouds in the story of the transfiguration (Luke 9:34–35) and the ascension (Acts 1:9, 11).

The *parousia* will be the final act of manifestation, revealing the glory of the divine presence. It will be the indescribable climax to the age-long revelation and unveiling of the majesty of God. He will appear in his everlasting glory to receive the worship and the honour which is his due (Revelation 5:11ff.; 7:10ff.).

2. It will be a *decisive* return. 'Then comes the end,' writes Paul in 1 Corinthians 15:24, when speaking of the return of the Lord. It will be the end, the terminal point for life in this world as it has been known throughout history. Jesus' own teaching carries a similar import (Mark 13:24ff.; Matthew 24:29ff.; Luke 21:25ff.; cf. also Revelation 1:7). At his coming the long march of the ages will be halted, the scheming and plotting of men will be ended, the last page of the history books will be written, the last act in the human drama played out and then the curtain will fall on the stage of time. Christ will come! (Luke 21:35.)

This means that the Lord's coming is the point towards which all human history is moving; it is the destination to which all life is headed and therefore an event whose significance is only finally comparable to the moment of creation at the beginning.

The coming of the Lord is therefore an event written into every human diary, every time-schedule, every work planner. It will be an event in the history of all men and women. It is not confined to the comparatively small number of people alive on earth at that precise moment, nor is it to be confined simply to the experience of the church. 'Every eye will see him' (Revelation 1:7) and 'every tongue' will acknowledge that he is indeed the Lord of all (Philippians 2:11). The Lord's return will be an event in the story of every human life whether or not they realize it now or are concerned about it in any way. Every human being is moving towards a rendezvous with the Lord at his coming.

3. It will be a *sudden* return. One of the recurring notes in the New Testament teaching about the Lord's return is its un-expectedness. 'The Son of man is coming at an hour you do not expect' (Matthew 24:44; cf. Malachi 3:1). In order to enforce this point Jesus reminded his disciples of the flood in the days of Noah. It took place with total unexpectedness. People were 'eating and drinking, marrying and giving in marriage' (Matthew 24:38). That is, they were carrying on with the normal, legiti-mate functions of life in the normal run of things with normal assumptions about tomorrow and next week and next year and all the usual planning for life in family and career and society when, completely unexpectedly, the flood came upon them. In other words the day the Lord returns will commence like any other day. The governments will be going about their business of governing, the business men will be in the midst of their planning, the workers will be setting about their work, and the whole round of social life will continue right up to the end. The whole normal human scenario, the planning for marriage, the expectation of a family, the plans for holiday, the dreams for promotion or a wage rise, the schemes for expansion and development, the anticipation of a sporting fixture or an evening out, will be the context upon which the *parousia* will burst with utter unexpectedness.

Jesus underlines the same point by four parables. One is of a master who goes away from home leaving his house in the care of his servants (Matthew 24:45–51; cf. Mark 13:34–36). His time of return is unknown and as a result the danger is that when he comes at the unexpected moment he will find the servants unworthily engaged, for 'the master of that servant will come on a day when he does not expect him and at an hour he does not know' (Matthew 24:50).

Another parable is of a householder who is burgled during the night (Matthew 24:43–44). Had he known when the thief was coming he would have been ready. But he didn't know and wasn't expecting it at that moment, and so suffered loss. The application is plain: 'be ready; for the Son of man is coming at an hour you do not expect' (24:44).

Another parable is about the ancient eastern Jewish custom of providing attendants for a bridegroom at a wedding. These girls met the bridegroom at his approach to the wedding celebration and accompanied him into the hall. In Jesus' story some did not prepare adequately and thus were not ready when the bridegroom arrived at an unexpected time (Matthew 25:1–13). 'Watch therefore, for you know neither the day nor the hour' (25:13).

The final parable is in a single phrase in Luke 21:3 – 'Take heed ... lest ... that day come upon you suddenly like a snare.' Just as the animal is caught precisely because it does not expect to be caught at that moment and is trapped by the snare, so the Lord's return will happen with devastating suddenness and surprise.

Paul uses very similar language virtually echoing that of Jesus cited above: 'the day of the Lord will come like a thief in the night' (1 Thessalonians 5:2; cf. Matthew 24:43; see also Revelation 3:3; 16:15). 'When people say, "there is peace and security," then sudden destruction will come upon them.' It will be, says Paul, like the commencement of a woman's birth-pangs (1 Thessalonians 5:3). The precise moment of the beginning of her labour pains is quite unpredictable. This is so, relatively speaking, even today with all our modern techniques for monitoring pregnancies, and therefore how much more sudden and unexpected in a society which predated the whole of modern medical development.

But perhaps the clearest reference to the unexpectedness of the Lord's coming is the statement of Jesus recorded in Matthew 24:36 and Mark 13:32 – 'But of that day or hour no one knows, not even the angels of heaven, nor the Son, but the Father only.' What is particularly striking is that in this verse Jesus expresses a claim for himself almost without parallel in the gospel records of Matthew or Mark. He claims to be in a different category and at a different level from all men, and from all the heavenly beings. He is the eternal Son of the Father. Yet he confesses that within the self-imposed limitations of his having become man he is also at that moment ignorant of the time of his glorious appearing. If incarnate godhead did not know the time, then it is clearly outside the capacity of any mortal to know it. The hour of the Lord's coming therefore cannot be known with any precision. It will be sudden and unexpected.

At this point it may be felt that the whole picture has not been presented. What about the whole business of the signs which are to precede the Lord's coming? Are they of no significance? After all, when the disciples asked Jesus about the time of his coming and the signs which would accompany it he did not dismiss their question (Mark 13:4). In fact he answered it at some length (Mark 13:5–37; cf. Matthew 24:4–25, 46). We will need to take account of this in the next chapter and show how the signs of the times fit into the whole picture. However, nothing which we shall conclude there can set aside the general point which the Bible plainly makes concerning the Lord's return. It will be sudden and unexpected.

The purpose of the Lord's return

The Bible has a lot to say about the things which Jesus will accomplish when he returns in glory, and we shall explore the most important of them in some detail in coming chapters. For the moment we shall simply list the main purposes of the Lord's return and make some limited comment on them.

1. The Lord's return will be *to complete the work of redemption*.

In 1 Corinthians 15:24 the 'end' which is equated with 'his coming' (verse 23) is when Christ has destroyed 'every rule and every authority and power'; for 'he must reign until he has put all his enemies under his feet' (verse 25). The *parousia* is therefore the conclusion of a process in which the enemies of God and his Christ are successively overthrown. It will be the completion of the whole age-long redemptive work of God.

This process of salvation began on the very heels of the fall (Genesis 3:15). It was carried into triumphant effect in the life, death and resurrection of the Lord Jesus and the continuing ministry of the Holy Spirit. It will be crowned by Jesus' appearing. At his coming the devil will be cast out (Revelation 20:2, 10; 2 Thessalonians 2:8–12; 1 John 3:8; Revelation 12:7–11) and all his evil schemes eternally destroyed. Christ comes as the 'last' or 'second' Adam to undo and overturn the sorry effects of the fall of the first Adam (Romans 5:12–21; 1 Corinthians 15:22, 45–47). In the return of Jesus all the promise and achievement of the Lord's first coming will burst into glorious fulfilment. The accuser of God's people will be banished (Revelation 12:7ff.), the curse of sin removed and a new eternal order will be inaugurated; a new heaven and earth in which God's original purposes for his creation will find their realization (2 Peter 3:1ff.; Romans 8:18ff.; Isaiah 2:1–4; 11:1–10; Psalm 2:1–9; 72; 45; Revelation 22:1–15).

In thinking of the Lord's return in this way it is important to avoid any separation of the second advent from the first. It is not that the first advent was somehow inadequate and that it now needs the second to do the job properly. The second advent is not like a second attempt at overcoming God's enemies made necessary by the inadequacies of the first. The two advents are simply distinguishable parts of one great, single, redemptive work of God. The second is implicit in the first from the very beginning. They belong together. They make up one single and whole act of redemption. Indeed the New Testament is concerned to assert that the essential victory over evil and sin and death was won at the first Easter (Matthew 28:18; John 12:31; Acts 2:32–33; Romans 8:34; 1 Corinthians 15:25; 2

Corinthians 2:14; Ephesians 1:20–22; Colossians 2:12; Hebrews 1:3; 2:14; 1 Peter 3:21b–22; Revelation 5:5–14). The work of Christ in his second advent is therefore to bring to their fullness the conquest and victory won decisively in his first advent.

2. The Lord's return will be *to resurrect the dead*. We will say more on this theme later. Here we note the link which Scripture establishes between the *parousia* and the resurrection of the dead. At his coming 'all who are in the tombs will hear his voice and come forth, those who have done good, to the resurrection of life, and those who have done evil, to the resurrection of judgment' (John 5:28–29). He is destined 'to judge the living and the dead ... by his appearing' (2 Timothy 4:1). Thus at the Lord's return all who have ever lived over the ages are to be called back to embodied life in some sense by the power of God operating through Christ at his coming (Mark 12:24ff.; cf. also Matthew 13:49; Luke 9:26; 19:15; John 6:39–40; 1 Corinthians 15:20–22; Philippians 3:20–21; 1 Thessalonians 4:16; Revelation 20:11ff.).

3. The Lord's return will be to *judge all men*. The second purpose, the resurrection of the dead, is clearly primarily with a view to this third purpose – that the dead having been resurrected might be brought to judgement. The two are inseparable. This aspect will occupy us again in a later chapter. At this point we note the clear biblical testimony to the fact of coming judgement. Perhaps the clearest New Testament reference is the one in 2 Timothy 4:1 cited above, as well as Acts 17:31 – God has appointed a day 'on which he will judge the world in righteousness by a man whom he has appointed.' Such is the unbroken testimony of the biblical writers. The Old Testament exposition of the Messiah's work is regularly cast in terms of his judging the wicked (cf. Deuteronomy 18:19; Psalm 2:9; Psalm 45:4–5; 110:5; Isaiah 11:4; 61:2; Malachi 3:1–3). In the New Testament the Lord will come to judge (Matthew 16:27; 25:14–46; 19:28; John 5:22, 27ff.; Acts 10:42; Romans 2:3–16; 3:5ff.; 1 Corinthians 4:5; 11:28ff.; 2 Corinthians 5:10; 2 Thessalonians 1:7ff.; Hebrews 6:1ff.; 2 Peter 3:10; Jude 14ff.; etc.). All men must appear before him at his coming.

Judgement is not confined to non-Christians. Christians will also face a judgement (Matthew 25:14–30; 25:31–46; Luke 19:12–27; Romans 14:10–12; 1 Corinthians 3:13–15; 2 Corinthians 5:10; 1 Peter 1:17; Revelation 20:12–13). There is no question that this judgement could put at stake the Christian's salvation for 'there is ... no condemnation for those who are in Christ Jesus' (Romans 8:1). If we believe in the Lord Jesus then his perfect righteousness stands to our account and God's wrath is eternally turned away from us. Anything else would be out of harmony with the joyous confidence and freedom before the Lord which the Christian is encouraged to enjoy. Christians' judgement will be in respect of their stewardship of the gifts, talents, opportunities and responsibilities which they have been given during their lives. Perhaps the spirit of this judgement is best conveyed by the reference to it in 1 Peter 1:17, '... you invoke as Father him who judges each one impartially'. It will be a fatherly judgement, and hence not one which will call in question the Christian's standing within the family of God. It will have all of a father's understanding and compassion and yet for all that it is clearly not to be disregarded or treated carelessly. This fatherly judgement will be exercised by the Lord at his coming.

4. The Lord's return will be *to ransom the church*. A number of scriptures speak of Christ's coming in relation to the deliverance of the people of God (cf. Matthew 24:22, 31; Mark 13:27; 1 Thessalonians 4:13–18; 2 Thessalonians 1:10; Revelation 21:1ff.). The Bible in several places refers to the persecution of the people of God as apparently being of particular intensity at the time of the Lord's return (Daniel 7:21; Matthew 24:12; 21ff.; Mark 13:19ff.). The Lord by his coming will deliver his people and ransom them from their enemies. But it will not be confined to those who are on earth at the time of the *parousia*. All those who died in faith in intervening centuries will also be taken to be 'with the Lord' at his coming. While they are already in a sense 'with him' (Philippians 1:23; see below, chapter 7) they are also waiting for the Lord's coming (cf. Revelation 6:9ff.) that they too may be given their new bodies (1 Corinthians

15:42–57; 2 Corinthians 5:1–5) and enter into the fullness of the life of the new age which Christ will inaugurate at his coming. Christ will come like a heavenly bridegroom to call his bride out of all the opposition, darkness and sin of life in this world, to the full and perfect fellowship and communion with him in the new age of glory (Revelation 21:1–4; 19:7–8; 22:1–5; Ephesians 5:21–33).

The time of the Lord's return

A further and important aspect of the Lord's return remains to be dealt with – the time of it. Some of what we have discussed in this chapter is relevant to this issue, but it obviously requires a much fuller treatment. There are also a number of quite complex though very interesting issues which have vexed Christian interpreters over the years, and we ought not to omit reference to these. We will take this material into the next four chapters. However, while very interesting and not without a certain importance, these issues are not *all* important even though we do need to take some account of them.

The fact that the Lord is coming is a far more important issue than questions of when it will all take place, or the precise nature of the events which will accompany his coming. He is coming – *that* is the great reality; exactly when and precisely how, though not unimportant in their way, are in the end secondary issues. Christ is coming, he is destined to reign in his eternal glory and to inherit the glory and honour of heaven and earth. That and nothing else is the substance of the Christian hope and that is the centre around which all the other aspects of the Last Things find their proper place.

3
THE SIGNS OF THE TIMES

There have been many attempts in the course of history to calculate the date of the *parousia*. There have also been lots of occasions when Christians have thought the end was going to come in their lifetime.

Lessons from history

As far as fixing the date goes, the year 1000 was an obvious one to go for. There was widespread speculation at the time that the end would come when the first millennium (period of 1,000 years) after Jesus' ministry on earth was completed. In the twelfth century an Italian monk called Joachim worked it out for sometime between 1200 and 1260. John Napier, the man who invented logarithms, put his method to work on dating the second coming and came up with a date between 1688 and 1700. In our own century a good number of interpreters used an alleged link-up between Luke 21:24 'the times of the Gentiles', and Daniel 4:16, 25, 32 with its reference to the 'seven times', to compute a time for the *parousia* early in the twentieth century. The first world war appeared to give the kind of apocalyptic atmosphere needed, and the declaration of a national home for the Jews added to the credibility of the interpretation. Other attempts were made when the second world war broke out, and again the political fate of Israel seemed to add confirmation. The Jehovah's Witnesses have the reputation for regularly coming up with the time of the end. So far they have had a try for 1874, 1914, 1915, 1975 and 1976, and we can no doubt expect a few more.

Quite apart from the actual prediction of the year of the Lord's return there have been numerous periods since the first century when Christians have believed that they were living in the last generation. Martin Luther the great reformer, for example, fully expected the Lord to come in his day. It would be a great mistake to imagine that people have never despaired about the state of the world until they arrived in the middle of the twentieth century. People were in fact despairing of the world before Christ was born. And there was certainly a deep despair in the world into which Jesus came. Daniel Defoe wrote in 1722:

> No age since the founding and forming of the Christian Church was ever like, in open avowed atheism, blasphemies, and heresies, to the age we now live in.

And some years later Bishop Butler could complain that

> it has come to be taken for granted that Christianity is not so much as a subject for enquiry; but that it is now, at length, discovered to be fictitious.

Writing in 1894 James Denney observed that

> one would think from the tone of current literature that no person with gifts above contempt is any longer identified with the gospel. Clever men we are told do not become preachers now – still less do they go to church.

The message of all this ought to be plain enough – caution! When some of the holiest, wisest and most knowledgeable and spiritually effective servants of God have got it wrong it is certainly time to tread carefully. However, equally it would be a mistake to dismiss this subject altogether – for the best of reasons, the Bible doesn't!

The signs according to Jesus

What are these signs? The best place to begin is with Jesus' teaching. In his reply to the disciples (what the scholars call 'the Olivet discourse' because it was given from the Mount of

Olives, see Matthew 24:3) Jesus identifies four general features of the period before his coming.

1. decline in religious faith: Mark 13:5-6, 21-22; Matthew 24:11-12.
2. the persecution and the world-wide witness of the church: Mark 13:9-11; 13:19.
3. wars and conflicts between the nations of the world: Mark 13:7-8; Luke 21:20f.
4. disturbances in the natural world: Mark 13:8; 24-25; cf. Luke 21:11.

However, the discourse is a bit more complicated than it may seem at first reading. The disciples in their question actually combined two questions. Jesus had just spoken of the destruction of the great temple of Herod which was the glory of the city of Jerusalem and of the Jewish religion. When they had recovered from the shock at such a prospect they asked him, 'Tell us, when will this be, and what will be the sign of your coming and the close of the age?' (Matthew 24:3). They asked about two things, the time of the destruction of the temple and the time of the Lord's return. Jesus' reply answers both questions, but in a way which weaves the two together, and it is here that the difficulties lie.

In Mark 13:14-20 (cf. Matthew 24:15-22) Jesus appears to be referring to a coming historical catastrophe in the lifetime and experience of the disciples which will involve the destruction of Jerusalem and its temple. The reference to the 'desolating sacrilege standing in the holy place' (Matthew 24:15) is a reference to the introduction of a heathen altar into the holy place in the Jerusalem temple by a pagan conqueror in 168 B.C. Jesus predicts a repetition of this. The fulfilment of Jesus' prophecy occurred in the terms in which he had predicted in A.D. 70 when the Romans recaptured Jerusalem following a Jewish rebellion. The city was put to the sword and the temple desecrated and burned down.

However, Jesus does not stop there, but links the coming judgement of God upon impenitent Israel in A.D. 70 with the final catastrophe at the end of the age which will precede his return (Mark 13:21–27; Matthew 24:23–31). Clearly in Jesus' mind the two events are closely related, the one leading directly into the other. In fact, nearly two thousand years now stretch between the two events, and we are in no position to say how much longer the gap will become. What are we to make of this?

Was Jesus mistaken?

Did Jesus get it wrong? Some have taken that view but it appears unwarranted, not merely because it would conflict with the rest of the New Testament evidence concerning his deity. Jesus himself professed ignorance of the time of his coming (Matthew 24:36) and there are a number of points within his address which show that he anticipated a real delay in his return (cf. Matthew 24:14, 26, 37–39, 42–44, 48–50; 25:5, 19).

How then do we explain this? The best answer would appear to be that in Jesus' mind the destruction of Jerusalem and the judgement of the Jews for their rejection of their Messiah are inextricably bound up with his return. We may recall the fact noted in the last chapter that one of the primary purposes of Jesus' return will be to execute judgement. Thus men's reaction to Christ belongs to the central theme of human history. It is the thing which determines the movement of the ages and God's sovereign ordering of human affairs. This point is also made by Peter (cf. 2 Peter 3:9): the delay in the Lord's return is due to God's longsuffering and patience with men to give them time to repent and turn to Christ. The same point is made when Jesus and Peter (Mark 13:10 and 2 Peter 3:12) both link the time of the Lord's return with the universal spread of the gospel, when people are given the opportunity to believe and be saved through Christ.

Thus human response to Christ is the central theme of history and helps to determine the unfolding of the purposes of God. The destruction of Jerusalem is therefore a genuine historical instance of the grace and judgement of God which will culminate at the end of the age in the return of Christ. We can put this conclusion more generally by noting the point made in the last chapter that the two comings of Jesus must be held together. His first coming and its rejection by the Jews is essentially bound up with the events of his second coming.

There is one other point to note about Jesus' teaching. It is immediately relevant to the people he addressed, the disciples. Jesus did not give them teaching which was irrelevant to them and intended only for a distant, unborn generation in the twentieth or thirtieth century, who would actually be alive at the time of the end. This is something which is a consistent feature of all the Bible's teaching about the Last Things, and which puts it in another world altogether from the star-gazers and horoscope merchants. It is always moral teaching. It is concerned with the way we are to live in the light of it. We will take up this point again in the last chapter. The importance of this is that the biblical teaching about the signs of the times is relevant to every generation of God's people. It is not just for those alive when the Lord comes. In other words being able to fit events into the prophecies is not the overriding thing. What really matters is how we live here and now in the light of the fact that God's judgements are abroad in history and that Christ is coming again in glory. The question of the precise time of that is not the primary thing for Jesus; the primary thing is, how does all this relate to my life and my conduct today?

The signs according to Paul

Paul refers to the theme in 2 Timothy 3. He teaches that 'in the last days there will come times of stress' (verse 1), and then proceeds to list the factors which will bring this about. There will be intense self-centredness with all its accompanying anti-social expressions in both family and society (verse 2–4). In religious life there will be outward form but no inner reality (verse 5). Significantly, Paul sees this whole movement of wickedness as already in operation in the persons of false teachers in his own day (verses 6–7), and as already expressed in the Old Testament period in the persons of Jannes and

Jambres, the Egyptian magicians who withstood Moses (verse 8; cf. Exodus 7:11).

In 2 Thessalonians he states that before the Lord's coming there will come 'the rebellion' and the appearing of 'the man of lawlessness' (verse 3). This person will so exalt himself as to claim deity (verse 4). He will be slain by Christ at his coming (verse 8).

From all this teaching of Jesus and Paul what may we conclude about the signs of the times?

Our own approach

In view of the complexity of these issues there is a temptation to leave the whole subject on one side and get on with the business of living the Christian life in the present. After all, the problems of today are so pressing and demanding that there is little time surely for sitting around counting up the signs of the times.

Actually this attitude is not so far from the correct one as it may at first seem. Two things may be claimed to support it. The first is the fact that in general Jesus did not encourage a 'signs of the times' mentality. In Luke 17:20 he states that 'the kingdom of God is not coming with signs to be observed' and he utterly refused to point to signs authenticating his ministry when asked to provide them (Matthew 12:38–39; 16:4; Luke 11:29; Mark 8:12). On occasion he did speak rather more positively of signs when rebuking the Pharisees for not reading them correctly (Matthew 16:3; Luke 12:56; cf. Luke 21:29ff.), and John's gospel sees Jesus' miracles as signs which point to his significance (John 2:11; 2:23; 3:2; 4:54; 7:31; 12:37; etc.). At first sight Jesus' attitude actually seems a bit ambiguous, but the point of it is that he was opposed to people who tried to avoid the moral and spiritual implications of his coming. The Pharisees and the other 'sign-seekers' were not really prepared to face up to the implications of Jesus' claims. Their interest in the signs was really only one of detached curiosity. Jesus was only prepared to perform signs and give evidence of the significance of his ministry to those who were prepared to alter their life-style in keeping with his claims.

We therefore need to be very sensitive to this danger today. It is only too possible for an interest in fulfilled prophecy to be detached from our desire to bring our lives fully into line with God's will for us. In fact, unless we are careful, this whole 'signs of the times' business can be a harmful rather than a helpful influence in our Christian lives, actually feeding aspects in our characters which are opposed to the Lord's claim upon us.

The second thing in the gospels which at first appears to reject all concern with the signs is the parable of Jesus in Matthew 24:45–51. The servant commended by his Lord when he returned was the one found busy at the tasks which the Lord had delegated to him. If our concern with the signs of the times leads to a neglect of the tasks and responsibilities of service which lie to our hands then we will fall under the Lord's condemnation. Paul has some pretty sharp things to say about Christians who neglect work and service (2 Thessalonians 3:6–13).

While these passages point out the dangers of speculative curiosity rather than moral obedience and committed service, they do not mean that we should write this whole area off. For one thing Jesus called upon his disciples to be watchful (Matthew 24:42; 25:13). He referred to the fig tree and its lesson, that when its fruit appears it is a sign that summer is near (Matthew 24:32–33).

Paul is also prepared to speak about certain events in relation to which the Lord's return will take place (2 Thessalonians 1–2). It will not happen at any moment, but only after the coming of 'the rebellion' and the 'man of lawlessness' (2:3). The Lord's return is therefore not a totally unpredictable happening which breaks in from the beyond without any sort of warning. Rather it stands in some kind of relationship to discernible events within history, and Paul is concerned that his readers should have some awareness of what these events are.

In the light of this we therefore cannot dismiss the kind of issue which the 'signs of the times' raises. However, we have already seen the need for extreme caution. This caution as far as our attitudes are concerned needs to be extended to a caution as far as the actual discerning and identifying of the signs are concerned.

Reasons for caution

1. We recall the passages which make clear the unexpectedness of the Lord's return when it does take place (Matthew 24:44, cf. Malachi 3:1; Matthew 24:50, 43–44; 25:13; Luke 21:34; 1 Thessalonians 5:2; Revelation 3:3; 16:15). Thus no study of the signs will in fact remove the sense of surprise, even among those who are faithful (Matthew 24:44). The whole attempt to find a detailed blueprint for the final days leading up to a precise prediction of the Lord's coming appears a doubtful procedure in the light of this.

2. Alongside the unexpectedness of the Lord's coming these passages assert directly the disciples' and their successors' ignorance of the time. He will come at an hour we do not know – 'you do not know on what day your Lord is coming' (Matthew 24:42; cf. 24:50; 25:13). This point is really the same as the first, but it makes it even more clearly. In Acts 1:7 Jesus says 'It is not for you to know times or seasons which the Father has fixed by his own authority.' Jesus says we simply do not and, by implication, will not know the precise time of his appearing.

3. In Matthew 24:36 (Mark 13:32) Jesus astonishingly states that even he at that moment does not know the time of his coming. What makes this confession the more surprising is that it comes in the context of a statement in which he shows an almost unparalleled consciousness of his divinity. If Jesus, in the perfection of his manhood and his unique knowledge of the Father and his will and purposes, is forced to admit his ignorance of the time of his coming, then clearly no man dare claim such a knowledge. This single statement of Jesus is a rock upon which all detailed timetables for the events of the last days inevitably founder. A real dose of scepticism is therefore not only allowable and prudent, it is in fact a reflection of the mind of Christ.

4. Another caution from the Scriptures arises in Peter's discussion of the delay in the Lord's coming in 2 Peter 3:1-10. In the course of it he points out that God's timescale is entirely different from ours: 'with the Lord one day is as a thousand years, and a thousand years as one day' (verse 8). Both sides of this equation need to be noted. Time for God has both an intensity ('one day is as a thousand years') and a brevity ('a thousand years is as one day') which cannot be known and appreciated by us. Therefore we should hesitate before committing God to our human timetables as though the passage of time as we discern it places him under any kind of obligation. He is Lord. His purposes will not fail. Jesus is Lord and destined to reign in eternal glory. Of these facts we need have no doubt whatever. But *how* God will bring this about and how his purpose precisely relates to our historical process and our measurements of time is quite another matter. Certainly God's purposes are not irrelevant to human history, as the fact that he became a man himself in history shows. But to claim a detailed knowledge of this relationship is surely unwarranted. God's timescale is not to be equated with ours.

5. There is also need for caution as far as the whole idea of the 'last days' is concerned. In Hebrews 6:5, 1 Corinthians 10:11 and Acts 2:17 the idea of the last days clearly refers to the entire period which began with the ministry, death and resurrection of Christ. The 'last days' is the entire period between the two comings of Jesus, when the kingdom of God has truly come but still awaits its full manifestation. The list of the features of the last days in 2 Timothy 3 should therefore be interpreted as features of life in the whole period between the comings of Jesus. Because the kingdom has come the 'end time', the final age, has already come upon us. We are therefore living in the last days, and so have all who have lived since Jesus came. In this sense therefore the signs of the end of the age are signs which will appear right through the history of the world between the two advents. What Jesus gives us are signs of the presence of the kingdom. In this sense the end is always near because Jesus is near. The real and decisive victory over the devil and all evil

powers has been attained already, and so nothing is preventing the final overthrow of evil except God's mercy which is holding back the final destruction of evil to give men the opportunity to hear the good news and come to repentance (2 Peter 3:9; Matthew 24:14). Therefore to assert that the coming of the Lord is at hand is always correct, right through the church age (Philippians 4:5; Revelation 22:20).

Finding the balance

Are we then to conclude that Jesus could conceivably return or have returned at any moment in the two thousand years since his ascension? No, that would not quite be true. In 2 Thessalonians 2:3ff. Paul is replying to those who are claiming that the final Day has already taken place. Paul's response is – that's wrong, because certain things have to happen first (verse 3). In other words the *parousia* stands in relationship to certain events within history. It cannot 'just happen' at any moment. What are these things which must happen first? We will examine them in more detail in the chapters which follow, but in general Paul teaches that there will take place a certain intensification of evil in the period before the Lord comes. In other words there will be a polarization of the forces of good and evil before the end. However, even this is not so precise that we can identify it beyond question, as is shown by the history of failed attempts already noted.

What then may we say in conclusion?

1. The really important factor is our moral attitudes – what we are, our desire to do the Lord's will and serve him with all we have.

2. The attempt to map out the details of the events in the last days and to try to predict the date and time of the Lord's return is misguided.

3. However, the other extreme of turning our backs on the whole question of the 'signs' is also wrong.

4. The correct attitude is one of watchfulness, recognizing that there will be a certain sharpening of the conflict between good

and evil before the end, though even that will not altogether escape the ambiguity of history. The Lord is always standing ready to come. The precise time lies in the perfect timing of God.

4
INTERPRETING PROPHECY

Much of the Bible's teaching about the Last Things occurs in what have become known as the 'prophetic' sections of the Bible. In the Old Testament this covers the entire concluding part from Isaiah through to Malachi. In the New Testament the material is less concentrated. Jesus' sermon on the Mount of Olives (Matthew 24–25; Mark 13; Luke 21) contains much straight-forward prophetic material, while 1 Thessalonians 4–5, 2 Thessalonians 2, and 2 Peter 3 are other major New Testament prophetic passages, and there are other briefer sayings of this type. These prophetic writings are a form of material which is not immediately familiar to us, so we obviously need to try to formulate the principles which should govern our interpretation of them. If we fail to do this we shall obviously be at the mercy of every whim of human imagination in our interpretation.

Principles to apply

How then ought we to interpret this biblical material? Are there any general principles to apply? There are three which are particularly important.

1. The way the New Testament interprets Old Testament prophecy should guide us in interpreting all biblical prophecy. The same Holy Spirit who inspired the Old Testament prophecies was active in the inspiration of the New Testament scriptures (2 Peter 1:21; John 14:26; Luke 24:44ff.). Thus we

have in the New Testament God's own commentary on the Old Testament prophetic passages. As we study these interpretations we shall be able to understand something of the mind of Christ in relation to prophetic interpretation.

When we study New Testament commentary on Old Testament prophecy we arrive at the following secondary principles:

(a) The Messiah of Old Testament prophecy is none other than the Lord Jesus Christ. All the Old Testament categories, Son of God, King after David's line, Suffering Servant, Son of man, righteous Branch, Prophet of God's people, are now seen as predictions and foreshadowings of Jesus Christ. Indeed 'all the promises of God find their Yes in him' (2 Corinthians 1:19–20).

The great focus of God's work which is foretold in the Old Testament has therefore come to fulfilment in Jesus. While there are still aspects which remain unfulfilled the major Old Testament predictions have now been realized. Thus the relation of Old Testament to New Testament may be expressed as 'promise-fulfilment'. In general the Old Testament prophetic passages have already received fulfilment in him who is the centre of God's saving purposes for the world.

(b) Materialist prophecies may well have a spiritual fulfilment. Many of the Old Testament predictions of Jesus Christ depict his ministry in terms of great material honour and prosperity. This is true in particular of those who see him as the inheritor of the glory of David's kingdom, such as the royal Psalms which depict the glories of Messiah's reign (cf. Psalms 45, 72). In fact the fulfilment shows that the riches of his reign are the riches of grace and mercy (cf. Ephesians 1:7–8; 2:7; etc.). His present reign is spiritual, not material.

(c) Prophecies which appear to refer to the prophet's own period may in fact refer to events in the distant future. Thus the prophecies concerning the Lord Jesus as the prophet who was to come (Deuteronomy 18:15ff.), of the righteous Branch (Jeremiah 23; 33; Zechariah 3:8), or Emmanuel (Isaiah 7:14), are all cast in a form which would seem to imply an immediate fulfilment. But this was not in fact so. We therefore need to beware of dogmatizing about the precise time of prophetic fulfilment. Prophetic oracles are often given in a form which leaps over generations and centuries of time. The future is foreshortened and appears virtually as the present moment.

(d) The kingdom of God which the Old Testament prophesies is in fact the kingdom of our Lord Jesus Christ. Just as Christ is the King in David's line so his rule is the kingly rule of God which the Old Testament predicts. The coming day of the Lord in which God will be truly known among his people and his blessing shared among them as never before is the kingdom which Jesus proclaimed had come near in his ministry. In the new covenant God would write his law on men's hearts and put his Spirit within them and cause them to obey him from the heart (Jeremiah 31:31ff.; Ezekiel 36:25ff.), and this is fulfilled in the mission of Jesus, through his death by which the new covenant was inaugurated (1 Corinthians 11:25) and the gift of the Holy Spirit (Acts 2:17ff.; cf. Joel 2:28–32).

As with the messianic fulfilment so with the messianic kingdom, materialist prophecies have a spiritual fulfilment. The blessings of Messiah's reign (cf. Isaiah 11:1–10; Psalm 72 etc.) which are cast in material terms refer in principle to the blessings of the kingdom of God which all who believe in Jesus have entered through faith, blessings of peace with God and each other, forgiveness of sin, the joy of the Lord's presence, security, guidance, fellowship, the hope of glory, and so on (cf. e.g. Romans 5:1–5). In Jesus and his kingdom of grace the promises to David find fulfilment (Psalm 89:3–4, 20, 24, 27–29; Isaiah 9:6–7; 2 Samuel 7:11–16) as Mary (Luke 1:32–33) and Zechariah (Luke 1:67–75) make plain.

(e) Many of the Old Testament prophecies concerning Israel are fulfilled in the church which is the new Israel. This principle applies at the primary point of the covenant made with Abraham which underlies the entire Old Testament hope. Paul insists in Romans 4 and Galatians 3 that the blessing of the nations which was the ultimate reference of the promise to Abraham is fulfilled in the universal church which is made up of believers among both Jews and Gentiles. In Acts 15:13–18 the

Council of Jerusalem approves such an application of the Old Testament prophecy concerning the rebuilding of the dwelling of David (Acts 15:16ff.; cf. Amos 9:11–12). Thus the old, hard distinction between Jew and Gentile is removed (Romans 9:24–26; 10:11–13, 19–21; Ephesians 2:11–22; Galatians 3:28; 6:15). The ceremonial distinction is also taken away, and the old Aaronic priesthood is rendered obsolete by Christ who is priest after the superior order of Melchizedek (Hebrews 7:1 – 10:18). The earthly temple in Jerusalem, the central shrine of Jewish worship, is replaced by the new sanctuary, God's dwelling in his people by faith (Ephesians 2:20ff.; John 2:13–22; 1 Peter 2:5; 1 Corinthians 6:19–20; Revelation 21:1ff.).

This principle raises several problems and we shall need to look more closely at the Bible's teaching about Israel in the next chapter. Here we make the simple point that, in general, the New Testament sees the Old Testament prophecies to Israel as having ultimate reference to the universal church.

2. The prophets spoke to their own day in uttering their prophecies as well as predicting events in the future. The study of the culture, the thought forms, the social customs and the geographical layout of the peoples of Palestine in the period covered by the biblical writings has shown how deeply these writings are embedded in their times. The prophetic writings are no exception to this rule. The prophets spoke in the thought-forms and images of their own day. They would have been understood, at least in their main ideas, by all their contemporaries. While God through his Spirit certainly enabled them to speak of things far beyond their own period they still couched their message in the ideas of their time.

This principle is familiar enough to anyone who has studied the subject of biblical inspiration. God's very words are given through the instrumentality of men in such a way that the outlook and personality of the human authors are not arbitrarily set aside. This truth, that the prophets were in this sense men of their time, has very far-reaching implications, for it means that if we are to understand their prophecies we have to try to begin where they were and learn all that we can about their period in order to unravel the meaning of their oracles. In saying this we need of course to avoid overstating it by implying that God's word through the prophets can only be known to the scholar who has studied Old Testament history. That is a dangerous mistake, for it effectively removes the Bible from the layman who then has to wait upon the scholar in order to hear God's word. Such a position can be a denial of the illumination of the Holy Spirit in the heart and mind of the simplest believer, enabling him to understand and grasp the truth of God's word. However, the danger of *overstating* this principle should not drive us to fail to state it at all. Here we are simply following out the classical Reformation principle of biblical interpretation, that the literal meaning, i.e. the one which arises from the immediate context, is the basis of any correct interpretation.

We therefore need to be prepared to listen to what the Old Testament historian has to say to us about the original meaning of the prophetic oracles. We may certainly retain our independence of his findings, but it is beyond dispute that reverent scholarship of this character is a basic tool in interpreting prophecies which, particularly in the Old Testament, often employ ideas and allude to customs which are utterly foreign to the modern western mind and experience.

This principle obviously imposes limits upon the degree to which we can find hidden meanings in the biblical prophecies. We must begin with the straightforward sense and work from there.

An illustration of this may be observed in Ezekiel's vision of the new temple. It is difficult to see what other language he could have used to convey in his day the message which God laid upon him and wished to express through him to the exiles in Babylon. The picture of a rebuilt temple in a restored land and with new sacrifices being offered all added up to a most powerful expression of God's faithfulness to Israel, even in exile. It gave the assurance, which subsequent events were to confirm, that God would restore his people to their land, and beyond that, that God had great and wonderful things to give to them and to all men through the new messianic kingdom.

Had Ezekiel spoken of the messianic kingdom in terms of its New Testament fulfilment (e.g. in the language of the letter to the Romans, or Ephesians) he would have been understood neither by his hearers nor even by himself. His prophecy is therefore of necessity couched in language drawn from the past history and immediate understanding of the people he addresses. To ignore this fact and to try and understand Ezekiel's teaching in terms of some future earthly theocracy fails completely to observe this basic principle of prophetic interpretation.

3. Biblical prophecies can have more than one level of fulfilment. It is a failure to grasp this which leads to a mistaken literalism at times. Thus while the prophets do speak to their own age and make predictions in terms of their immediate situation, their prophecies can also have reference to events hundreds, even thousands of years later.

Thus the Emmanuel prophecy in Isaiah 7 probably had reference in the first instance to a prediction in the prophet's own lifetime. But it was also, unknown to that generation, a prophecy concerning the coming Messiah. Thus Abraham was blessed in the prospect of the inheritance of the land of Canaan by his seed. This came to fulfilment in succeeding generations, and yet as Paul argues in Romans and Galatians, the full terms of the promise are realized in the world-wide people of God in the Christian church.

This foreshortening whereby events in the far distant future are superimposed upon events in the present or immediate future is, as we have seen, reflected in Jesus' prophetic teaching in Mark 13, where the fall of Jerusalem in A.D. 70 is bound up with the events at the Lord's return. This is a prophetic technique which modern Christians find difficult to come to terms with. We are trained to think in either/or terms; either this prophecy refers to the prophet's own day or it refers to later history. The Bible, however, shows us that it is not impossible for it to refer to both.

4. The prophets employ images, figures of speech, and even symbols in order to convey their message. There is a vividness and freedom about prophetic writing which makes it different

from the normal language of every day. Certainly many of the prophetic books refer or allude to historic events in their time. Some sections are straightforward narrative. Alongside this, however, are passages where the imagination takes flight and we encounter bewildering images and notions. There is in other words a poetic strain in prophecy. Just as we do not expect poetry to be literally true so we ought not to try and press prophetic oracles into literal interpretations which they were never intended to express.

Apocalyptic literature

Let us now turn in particular to Daniel and Revelation, the two books in the Bible which have exercised the greatest influence on Christian thought about the events at the end. These two books show more clearly than others a literary kinship to the form of writing known as apocalyptic.

This name is given to a loosely defined group of writings among the Jews dated mostly from the last two centuries B.C. and the first century A.D. There are something under twenty of these writings. A few of them appear in the Apocrypha to the Old Testament. The apocalyptists have much in common with the prophets and the line between the two is not always easy to draw. The apocalyptic writings, however, do have certain special features.

1. These writings claim to be 'revelations'. That is what the word 'apocalypse' actually means. They claim to be God-given visions.
2. Closely allied to the first point is the use made in apocalyptic writings of symbolism. These writers do not use straightforward language, but couch their message in imagery which is almost wholly foreign to contemporary man. Beasts, seals, mountains, horns and especially angels all appear freely in the apocalyptic literature. Sometimes the meanings of the symbols are made clear. Often they are left obscure. The symbolic use of numbers is another typical apocalyptic feature.
3. These writings are filled with a sense of pessimism about the present. They look for a future solution to man's problems

in terms of a great and violent action or series of actions on the part of God which will bring about the annihilation of his foes and the deliverance and vindication of his oppressed people. 4. The apocalyptists, like the prophets, were concerned to predict the future, but their emphasis was somewhat different. The prophets spoke of the future as it related to the present. Their message was essentially addressed to their immediate hearers. They spoke as preachers addressing a living congregation. Even if the events were beyond the congregation's lifetime they were not irrelevant to their present situation and their immediate decisions. The apocalyptists on the other hand pushed their message wholly into the future and spoke of events which lay beyond human history in the strict sense.

Neither Daniel nor Revelation are straightforward apocalyptic writings. A number of the typical features of that literature are not present, but many features certainly *are* present and therefore we are bound to take these into account when we come to interpret these books. A failure to recognize this literary context for these books has led to all sorts of misinterpretation. This is particularly true when we come to the symbolism of these writings.

The significance of these two books, particularly the book of Revelation, has been so great as far as the shaping of people's view of the Last Things is concerned that we shall require to give a special section to the question of the interpretation of Revelation.

The book of Revelation

This book is on any reading the most difficult to interpret of the whole biblical literature. The great reformer John Calvin was so persuaded of its difficulties that it was the only biblical book which he did not attempt to write a commentary on. Certainly when we read some of the weird and wonderful notions which have claimed the authority of this book in their support it is difficult not to feel a strong sympathy with Calvin. However, God has inspired this book as surely as any other in the canon, and there are great truths embedded in it which we miss to our great impoverishment.

How may we interpret it? Four main lines of interpretation of the book of Revelation have been followed.

1. *Futurist:* this assumes that the relevance of the prophecies lies entirely in the end of the age and has nothing to do with the time in which John was living. The book therefore concerns events in the last days, understood as the days immediately preceding the *parousia.* Sometimes those who take this view confine it to chapters 4–22 and preface it with an historicist interpretation of chapters 1–3 (see below).

2. *Historicist:* this sees the book as a panoramic disclosure of events across the ages from the first century until the return of Christ. Some interpreters take the entire book in this manner, others note the three series of plagues (cf. seals, trumpets, bowls, chapters 6–19) and take this to imply a history in triplicate, the same ground being covered three times from different perspectives. A sharply modified form of the historicist position sees the book as divided into seven sections, each of which covers the same span of time, namely from the first to the second coming of Christ. Thus the whole period of the church is covered seven times with a mounting climax of judgement and blessing towards the final section.

3. *Preterist:* this regards the entire relevance of the prophecy to lie in the lifetime and immediate future of the author and his readers. This third approach is that taken by most recent scholars. It variously relates the book to historical events and figures within John's own period or to literary sources and images in the Old Testament and other apocalyptic literature.

4. *Idealist:* in reaction to all the other schools and the confusion which has surrounded the interpretation of this writing, this approach sees the whole thing as a kind of highly imaginative poetic composition designed simply to convey to suffering Christians the inspiration to persevere to the end. It interprets the book as having no significant relationship with history or the events of the end.

We need to weigh these approaches and determine which appears most in keeping with the book, with the rest of biblical teaching and the overall message and purpose of Scripture.

It would appear that no single approach is wholly satisfactory. The traditional historicist interpretation appears to have least in its favour in those interpretations which lead to the drawing up of massive charts tracing the development of world history over the ages. This whole business is simply foreign to the Bible and its message, and breathes more of the atmosphere of the horoscope and the astrologer than the 'glorious gospel of the blessed God' or the sane humanity of Jesus and the apostles. This method in its developed form stands self-condemned by the fact that its exponents have not been able to agree on which historical events are depicted, and one would have thought it not unreasonable to require unanimity on the major outlines at least.

It is again surely indicative of the highly subjective nature of this enterprise that in most cases it is events of western European history which God is apparently interested in and not those in the rest of the world! On the positive side the historicist school may be said to affirm the relevance of the book of Revelation for every generation, and if purged of the kind of excess mentioned above, can have real value where it uses spiritual principles rather than historical events as the key to interpretation.

The futurist approach has the value of taking the predictive element seriously. We cannot ignore the fact that although the book of Revelation is certainly an apocalyptic writing, it also claims to be a prophetic book and to be concerned with matters which lie in the historical future. The preterist approach, although there is much to commend it, often refuses to take this future dimension seriously. If the message of the book does refer in some sense to the events of the end time, then clearly some degree of future reference is present. The weakness of this futurist approach, however, is its failure to anchor interpretation in the setting of the author and his readers. It makes the book relevant to the generation immediately preceding the Lord's return, whichever generation that may be, at the price of making it completely irrelevant to the generation to which it was addressed. This is surely mistaken and in conflict with sound principles of interpretation.

The preterist approach avoids some of the excesses of the other views, and its primary concern, to interpret the book out of the time of its composition, is surely foundational and correct. It needs, however, to be supplemented in the sense noted above, to permit it to be referred to the future as well as the present, and to speak concerning events at the time of the return of the Lord.

The idealist view must be rejected in its assumption that there is no real significance in the imagery of the book, but it is no doubt correct in its concern to stress the *spiritual* message of the book in the setting of its readers.

The symbolism in Revelation

We have already made reference to the link between Revelation and apocalyptic literature. This is particularly important for the interpreter when he comes to make sense of the bewildering imagery of the book. Thus for example in apocalyptic literature beasts are commonly symbols for people, horns for kings and stars or men for angels. Perhaps supremely important in this regard is the fact that in apocalyptic literature numbers are almost always employed symbolically. The numbers 3, 4, 7, 10, 12 and multiples of them abound. The number 70 is also very common. Apocalyptic writers loved tidy numerical schemes and the use of patterns of recurring numbers is a feature of their systems.

The interpreter of Revelation recognizing this literary background will therefore not be put off by the often grotesque figures and personages he meets in its pages, recognizing them as symbolic figures. He will also learn not to take numbers literally, but also see them as a kind of code for other ideas and realities.

The message of Revelation

What then is Revelation all about? John writes against the backdrop of the present and imminent persecution of the infant church in Asia Minor, with its aggressive emperor worship and antipathy to the Christian claims for Christ. He writes to encourage the beleaguered church by showing them how the struggle in which they are engaged is part of an age-long warfare between God and the demonic realm which will continue through history to a climactic finale at the culmination of history and the *parousia* of the Lord. In this struggle, despite all appearance to the contrary, Christ is victor and Lord, and this will be manifest at his glorious future appearing. What then in essence is the message of this book? One may delineate three elements.

First, it asserts that faith is triumphant. In face of all the antagonistic forces – Rome, the beast, the antichrist, or whatever – it is finally indestructible. All these enemies will be laid low and the Lamb will be victorious in the end.

Secondly, judgement is inevitable. The language which John uses to convey this point is horrific at times, but he is trying to describe in such literary forms as were at his disposal what is finally indescribable, and there can be no question that he succeeded under the Spirit's inspiration in conveying the point powerfully enough. Evil and all who practise it, particularly in their persecution of the saints of God, are destined for fearful and final judgement.

Thirdly, and more by implication, Christianity presents the true view of history. Human history is an onward progression to a final goal at the return of the Lord and the inauguration of a new heaven and earth. We do not therefore look to Revelation for a detailed plan of the last times, but we do find expressed in memorable language principles which are true to the whole history of the people of God in their struggle against evil and Satan, a struggle which will intensify in some ways towards the end of the age.

5

TWO PROBLEM ISSUES

Antichrist

One of the main personages associated with the Lord's return is the antichrist. Biblical references to this occur most clearly in John's letters. He refers to 'antichrist' and the 'spirit of antichrist' as something about which his readers have already been taught (1 John 2:18; 2:22; 4:3; 2 John 7). It is already present and at work; indeed he says there are 'many antichrists'. The appearance of these antichrists are a clear sign that 'it is the last hour' (1 John 2:18). The thing which marks them out is their teaching. They 'deny the Father and the Son' (2:22), they refuse to 'confess Jesus' (4:3) and refuse to 'acknowledge the coming of Jesus Christ in the flesh' (2 John 7).

Paul does not use the title 'antichrist' but most interpreters see the teaching of 2 Thessalonians 2 as belonging to the same subject. There Paul mentions the coming of 'the man of lawlessness [*or* sin]' (verse 3). This person is destined to appear before Christ returns. He will be the one who 'opposes and exalts himself against every so-called god and object of worship' and 'takes his seat in the temple of God, proclaiming himself to be God' (verse 4). He will be destroyed 'by the appearance and coming' of the Lord Jesus Christ (verse 8).

Six, six, six
The third element of biblical teaching about the antichrist is more controversial. It occurs in the apocalyptic strand, Daniel and Revelation. Daniel 7:20–21 refers to a 'horn which had eyes

and a mouth that spoke great things, and which ... made war with the saints, and prevailed over them, until the Ancient of Days came'. Revelation 13:1–18 is claimed to be a similar allusion, where a grotesque beast comes out of the sea (verses 1–4), blasphemes God's name and is given universal authority (verses 5–10). It has 'a human number', six hundred and sixty six (verse 18). It is overthrown by the word of God and the armies of heaven (19:19–21).

On the basis of these passages numerous attempts have been made over the years to identify this 'man of lawlessness' or 'antichrist'. Nero, the Roman emperor, was thought to be the antichrist in the early centuries. Indeed there is a good case to be made for thinking that he *is* the figure which inspired John's description in Revelation 13 (see above on the interpretation of the book of Revelation). The Reformers, particularly Martin Luther, saw the antichrist as the Pope in Rome. This view was given plausibility by the fact that another strange embodiment of evil in Revelation 17 and 18, Babylon the 'mother of harlots', is fairly obviously a symbol for the city of Rome (cf. 17:9). Other great dictators or military leaders such as Napoleon, Bismarck, the Kaiser, Mussolini and Hitler have all appeared in the role. More recent contenders have been Stalin, Kruschev and Mao Tse-Tung.

The appearance of this figure with his secret number is claimed by many to be one of the clearest marks of the last days. However the sheer number of those who have been so identified in the past has tended to lead to a healthy scepticism in some quarters and, regrettably though understandably, sometimes even to the discrediting of the whole idea.

Antichrist today

In trying to interpret this biblical teaching it is wise to recall that the clearest references to antichrist are those in John's writings. John admits to the idea of an antichrist who is to come and whose coming is a sign of the 'last hour' (1 John 2:18), but he informs his readers that in fact it has already happened, 'many antichrists have come; therefore we know that it is the last hour.' According to John's teaching, therefore, antichrist is not to be confined to one unique figure but is a spirit which attaches to a whole group of people whose presence is a feature of the whole period of the last days. We have already seen that the idea of the 'last days' is to be referred to the whole period between the two comings of Christ. Therefore the spirit of antichrist is already in the world and will continue through history until Christ returns.

It is correct on the basis of 2 Thessalonians 2 to anticipate a final and climactic embodiment of the spirit of antichrist prior to the Lord's return. But whether we should spend time attempting to identify him is doubtful in view of the mistakes so regularly made in the past. And whether the Daniel and Revelation references are relevant, and what exactly we should learn from them even if they are, are matters where dogmatism is out of place.

What then do we do with this idea? We use the principle of interpretation which states that the obscure should be interpreted in the light of the clear. What *are* clear are the references in John's letters. Antichrist refers to a spirit already abroad in the world. It is a spirit which denies the true God and denies the Christian claim that Jesus Christ is God manifest in the flesh.

If we understand the antichrist in essentially *this* form, we have one tremendous advantage over the alternative business of identifying some living figure with the secret number six, six, six – which often has more in common with almanacs and crystal balls than the strong, sane, moral religion of the Bible. The advantage is that it makes the question of the antichrist immediately relevant to the church in *every* age. It is no longer confined to the single generation when Christ returns, which on any computation is the merest fraction of the whole people of God across the ages. The idea of the antichrist becomes a call to vigilance in the church today, and in every 'today', against all that would deny the truth of God and the full deity and true humanity of his eternal Son.

It is particularly significant that John speaks of these influences in his own day as having originated in the church itself (cf. 1 John 2:19 'they went out from us ...'). We need to clear away therefore something of the eerie and mysterious atmosphere which has surrounded this notion so often in the past and really bring it down to earth and see it as a call to faithfulness to the truth of God which has been delivered to the church; a call to the propagation and defence of the full biblical faith, and in particular its doctrines of God and the person of Christ. In support of this we may appeal to the admittedly difficult passage in Revelation 13, and keep before us the fact that the number of the beast is a '*human* number'. The power of the beast is therefore to be confronted on the *human* plane in doctrine propagated by human teachers.

The instinct which has led people to attempt to identify the antichrist with figures throughout history is not wholly mistaken. In one sense these identifications have all been correct in their way. For every denial of God manifests the spirit of antichrist, whether it be the formal denials of the false teachers or the implicit denials of the great dictators and all who aspire to divine authority and despise and destroy human life. That spirit is certainly abroad in the world today, and if we belong to Christ we are called to confront it. The sign of antichrist is therefore a sign to be reckoned with by every church and every Christian.

If an antichrist arises in our time or in the next generation whose denial of God and Christ assumes something of the impressive form which Paul alludes to in 2 Thessalonians, then we may feel some justification for lifting up our heads because our redemption has drawn near (cf. Luke 21:28). In the meantime we are not to be idle but rather by life and witness confront the powers of antichrist abroad in the world in our generation.

Israel

Another 'sign' which lies right at the heart of discussion about the Lord's return is the nation of Israel. The Bible clearly shows the way in which God chose this nation to be the historic channel of his purposes in the world (Genesis 12:3; 18:18; 22:18; 26:4; 28:14; Isaiah 43:8–10; 49:6). To them, as Paul states, belonged 'the sonship, the glory, the covenants, the giving of the law, the worship, and the promise' as well as the patriarchs (Romans 9:4–5). To Israel came the world's Saviour, Jesus Christ. In this sense as Jesus remarked 'salvation is from the Jews' (John 4:22).

In spite of all this Israel rejected God's calling by crucifying the Messiah when he came to them. Thus God's salvation was turned outwards to the Gentiles. This is what Paul calls the 'mystery hidden for ages', that 'God chose to make known how great among the Gentiles are the riches of the glory of this mystery' (Colossians 1:26–27), and 'how the Gentiles are fellow heirs, members of the same body, and partakers of the promise in Christ Jesus through the gospel' (Ephesians 3:6). We have earlier noted the way in which the New Testament writers freely apply the promises addressed to Israel in the Old Testament to the church in the New Testament (cf. Acts 15:13–18; Romans 4; 9:24–26; Galatians 3; 6:15; Ephesians 2:11–22; Hebrews 7:1 – 10:18; 1 Peter 2:4–10).

Has Israel a future?

Has God then finished with Israel? Is the time of Israel's significance confined to that period in history between the call of Abraham and the crucifixion? Some believe so, and indeed this view appears to underlie most evangelical thinking and preaching.

Others, however, are not so convinced, and see Israel as having a future role in God's purposes. They believe that the Jews are destined to play a highly significant part in the events which will immediately precede the return of Christ. As we shall see, this question of the future of Israel in God's purposes is a complex one and there are a variety of positions which have been adopted.

Twentieth-century pointers?

For those who believe in a future role for Israel in God's

purposes two political events in this century are seen as of tremendous significance. The first was the Balfour Declaration of 1917 whereby Palestine was declared a national home of the Jewish people. The second was the founding of the state of Israel in 1948. This restoration to the Jews of their former territory is alleged to be the fulfilment of the predictions of a number of Old Testament passages (Isaiah 11:11ff.; Zechariah 8:1–8; Jeremiah 30:24 – 31:6; Amos 9:14–15; Isaiah 35:1–2; 61:4). It is also seen as the fulfilment of Jesus' words in Luke 21:24 concerning the end of the 'times of the Gentiles' during which Israel will be 'trodden down' (cf. Matthew 19:28; Galatians 6:16; Romans 11:26). As a 'sign of the times' the return of the Jews to Palestine takes on a tremendous significance by this approach, for it implies the nearness of the second advent.

But is this correct? There certainly appear to be some grounds for questioning it. Many of the passages which speak of the restoration of the Jews appear to refer to the immediate historical context in the Old Testament, viz. their return from exile in Babylon (Jeremiah 29:14; Daniel 9:2; Deuteronomy 30:1–10; 1 Kings 8:46–52; Ezekiel 36:17–19, 26–28; Hosea 11:10–11). It is said that the restoration of the people from the Babylonian exile cannot be the correct fulfilment since that return to the land involved only two of the twelve tribes, the two comprising Judah. The other ten had been earlier deported by the Assyrians. However, this objection is in turn invalidated by the fact that the Bible in its later stages does not hesitate to see the nation restored from Babylon as the historic embodiment of God's purpose for the entire people of God (cf. Ezra 6:17; Ezekiel 37:15–28; Matthew 19:28; Luke 1:5; 2:36; Acts 26:7; James 1:1; Revelation 7:1–8; 21:12).

Further these Old Testament promises of restoration are made to a remnant of the whole nation who have faith in the Lord; they are not made to the nation as a whole in their unbelief. In several passages it is made plain that before the people will be restored to their land they will return to the Lord (Deuteronomy 30:2–3, 9–10; 1 Kings 8:47–50; Jeremiah

18:5–10; Hosea 11:10–11). This condition was certainly not met in the events of this century, but *was* met by those who returned from Babylon (cf. Ezra 3:4–5, 10–11; 6:16–22; 7:10; 8:35; 10:11–12; Nehemiah 1:4–11; Haggai 1:12ff.).

Similarly Jesus' words in Luke 21:24 appear simply to imply that Jerusalem will be 'trodden down' in the sense that the Jews will be removed from their central place in the redeeming purposes of God until the end of the present age, i.e. the period during which the gospel is taken to the ends of the Gentile world. The word 'until' in this verse has the same force as it has in Revelation 2:25, 'hold fast ... until I come.'

Will all Jews be saved?

Do we conclude then that the Jews have no place in God's purpose since their rejection of the Messiah? Certainly the case for claiming that the Israeli state as it presently exists has a place is unproven. But what of the Jews as a religious community, the people as a whole, including the great majority who do not live in Palestine?

Discussion of this question is largely bound up with the interpretation of several New Testament passages of which Romans 11:26 is supremely significant. The way in which we interpret this verse will largely determine how we see Israel in relation to the future. The important words are: 'all Israel will be saved.'

At first sight this phrase read within its immediate context, Romans 11:24–32, appears to assert not only the continuation of the nation of Israel within God's purposes but in fact a future act of mercy on God's part by which the entire nation will be restored to God, including by implication those multitudes of individual Jews who over the centuries have rejected him, and including indeed those who were the historic instruments of Jesus' crucifixion. Is this the correct view?

When we look at the larger context of Romans 9–11 the picture becomes less clear. Paul's general argument in these chapters is that the apparent rejection of the gospel by Israel which has been the means of the blessing of the Gentiles, is not an unqualified rejection. There is a group within the historic nation who have responded to the gospel, just as there was in the Old Testament period itself a distinction between those who believed and those who did not (9:6–29). The basis of this difference is not an arbitrary counsel of God but their acceptance or rejection of his mercy (9:30–10:21). But God has not given Israel up (11:1) as the presence of a believing company of Jews within the church shows (11:2–6). The fact that God has used the rejection of Jesus by the Jews to bring blessing to the Gentiles should have three results for Gentiles.

1. They should reflect that if the rejection of Israel has been the means of such blessing for the Gentiles, then if they should in fact turn again to God in faith the potential for blessing would be greater still (verses 12–16).

2. They should 'stand in awe' (verse 20) in recognition of the fact that if God has rejected his chosen people through their unbelief there is no ground for presuming upon their own standing with him. They need to rest wholly upon his mercy and grace (verses 17–22).

3. They should recognize the power of God in his dealings with his people, and that he is able to renew Israel again (verses 23–24).

So, Paul concludes, what has happened is that 'a hardening has come upon part of Israel, until the full number of the Gentiles come in, and so all Israel will be saved ... for the gifts and call of God are irrevocable' (25–26, 29).

What is Paul asserting here? There are four general ways of understanding him, though even these will need to be qualified at points. In fact the issues here are far from finally decided and it is wise to avoid undue dogmatism. We will attempt some kind of conclusion, but the reader will be disappointed if he expects a tidy solution.

A: *All means all*

Position A is to take the words 'all Israel' at face value. This view itself has several forms. First there is the notion that the whole race of Jews will be saved in the end (the position we outlined earlier). This has the advantage of keeping Paul's meaning for 'Israel' consistent through the passage. By 'Israel' he means the whole nation.

However, several difficulties arise here. First, there is the question of the basis upon which all these Jews are received by God. The whole burden of Paul's case in Romans 9–10 is that Israel has passed under judgement because it has failed to seek God on the basis of his grace, and that only on that basis have those who have been saved within the nation found their deliverance. It would be astonishing if Paul in Romans 11 were to reverse that whole point and champion a situation where salvation was dependent upon national identity. Surely then God's mercy would appear arbitrary indeed.

Another difficulty in this interpretation is that it requires us to deny any future judgement for those who in Israel's history were particularly noted by the Bible for their wickedness. Are then the company of Korah (Numbers 16), or Achan (Joshua 7), or Absalom (2 Samuel 15), or Jezebel (1 Kings 21), or Amon (2 Chronicles 33:21ff.), or Judas and those who plotted the crucifixion, all to be saved in the end? Such would surely make nonsense of the seriousness of the biblical teaching on the coming wrath of God. Besides, Paul himself argues in quite another manner in 1 Corinthians 6.

Finally, when this view is combined with one which sees the present Israeli state as the object of the biblical prophecies, then it introduces into considerations of Israeli activity in the Middle East a pro-Israeli bias which is out of keeping with the strict justice of God's dealing with men and nations. Like all modern states Israel has done, and will do both good and evil, right and wrong, and like all states she is responsible in the end to the judgement of the moral character and law of God.

Thus the whole attempt to understand Romans 11:26 in terms of a future national and racial restoration of Israel appears misplaced, and even fraught with serious moral implications.

Position A, however, is capable of a modification which makes it much more tenable. This would reject the idea of 'all Israel' as meaning the total national population in every generation.

Rather it sees Romans 11:26 as teaching that before the Lord's return there will come, through the mercy of God alone, a great world-wide turning of the Jews to their Messiah. Judaism will recognize Christianity as its true and rightful inheritance, and hence 'all Israel' in the sense of 'the nation as a whole' will find salvation. Thus within the limits of human history God's purposes and calling and election of Israel will find historic vindication (11:29). This view does not require the thought that every single individual Jew will be saved, or that redemption will come to those who over the ages have repudiated Christ or those who in the Old Testament period have rejected God's covenant and his law.

A form of this view was held by numbers of the English Puritans and their theological successors. They believed on the basis of Romans 11 that the church should confidently expect a great turning to Christ on the part of the Jews before the end of the present age, and that this would in turn be the means of great world-wide blessing for the church and its mission (cf. 11:12–15).

The important distinction made and preserved in these modifications of the 'national' understanding of *all Israel* is that the basis of salvation will be the grace of God in the gospel. It is a belief in Christ as Messiah which will bring the blessing of salvation. This, of course, enables us to preserve the consistency of Paul's argument that salvation, whether for Jew or Gentile, is by grace through faith.

B: *All means Christian Jews*
Position B understands 'all Israel' to imply 'all within Israel who believe'. Paul is here stating that in the mercy of God there is a saved remnant even among the Jews who have as a nation rejected Christ. There is a 'fulness of Israel' i.e. a totality of those called by God and brought to faith in Christ. All of these will be saved, none will be lost. Verse 25 is thus seen as equivalent to the 'fullness of Israel' in verse 12 where Paul has distinguished between Israel as a whole and 'the elect' within Israel (verses 7–10). Paul's hope was never more than that

'some' of his fellow Jews might be saved (verse 14). This interpretation would appeal to the fact that right at the beginning of
this discussion Paul distinguishes between those who are
Israelites by natural descent and those who are true Israelites
through faith (9:6–13). A similar interpretation of 'Israel' in
Galatians 6:16 might also be urged in support.

The weakness of this position is simply that it requires a
special meaning for 'Israel' which does not accord with eleven
out of the twelve uses of the term in these chapters. There is
also the difficulty of harmonizing it with 11:28, where Paul
speaks of Israel as 'beloved for the sake of their forefathers',
a clearly national reference.

C: *All means the church*

Position C argues that 'all Israel' refers to the wholeness of the
one people of God, both Jews and Gentiles who believe in
Christ. Thus 'Israel' is a synonym for the church. While this
has to face the difficulty of Paul's terminology in this whole
section (see criticism of position B above) it can appeal to a
rather richer biblical support. Galatians 6:16 can certainly be
read in this sense. It is difficult to sustain a meaning in that
passage which would require 'Israel' merely to equal the nation.

Further there is the whole weight of biblical testimony to the
effect that the church is the inheritor of the promises to Israel.
Israel as a nation is set aside. Further, a case can be made
from the construction which Paul uses which would support this
view: 'until the full number of the Gentiles come in, and *so*
[by virtue of the full number of Gentiles being saved] all Israel
will be saved.' Thus the meaning of Israel in verse 26 is defined
by the reference to 'the full number of the Gentiles' in the
preceding phrase. The grammatical and linguistic evidence here
however is not conclusive, so it cannot be cited as proof of
this interpretation; on the other hand it is a genuine possibility.

D: *All is Paul's hope*

There is a further view which in distinction from all the others
questions whether Paul is thinking of the future at all. The

whole debate concerns his hopes and motives as a Christian evangelist, who yearns for the salvation of his people (9:1–3) and who is confronted nonetheless by the mystery of their unbelief and rejection of their historic destiny. Romans 11:26 then expresses his hope with respect to his witness among them and his confidence in the ability of God to renew and restore his ancient people. Paul is not here gazing into any crystal ball or delivering the contents of some divine revelation he has been given about the future turn of events before Christ returns. He is simply giving expression to the burden of his own prayers and his confidence that God will yet in Paul's own day and even through his own ministry turn the tide of faith among his fellow countrymen and lead Israel back to her historic destiny.

There is a salutory relevance about this approach. It allows us to interpret the phrase in a manner which would have given it a sharp relevance to Paul's readers. Nor can we ignore the fact that the whole thing *is* introduced (9:1–3) in terms of Paul's own longing. This approach also has the commendable value of linking the section more immediately to the rest of Romans, since it has to be admitted that most discussions of these chapters approach them as if they were a separate letter of Paul with nothing other than an accidental connection to chapters 1–8.

Towards a conclusion

The reader should reflect upon all these possibilities. The only one which I find clearly unacceptable is position A in a national-political form. The difficulties of understanding 'Israel' in a sense other than 'the nation as a whole' however are real on a careful reading of the passage, and so positions B and C are not entirely satisfactory on that account, though position C probably meets this objection better than B. D is not without some attraction, as has been indicated.

On the whole I incline to position A in its modified form, but this appears a clear case where undue dogmatism should be ruled out. Let every man be persuaded in his own mind.

What then may we say about Israel? While the existence of

the nation of Israel is in its own way a witness to God's preserving mercy, it is to be doubted whether the present Israeli state has anything particular to do with events leading up to the return of Christ. A pro-Israeli bias in political judgements is therefore unwarranted and indeed may be a tacit denial of the justice of God to which the Bible bears unwavering witness. In the light of Romans 11:26, however, it may be that we should hope for a significant future turning to the Lord Jesus Christ on the part of many Jewish people, with resulting blessing for the world-wide church.

6
THE MILLENNIUM

The essential idea of the millennium is that there will be a glorious kingdom of Christ on earth after his return and prior to the coming of the eternal order. This lies at the heart of many of the divergences of opinion over the Bible's teaching about the second advent. The word comes from the latin term for one thousand, *mille*. The Greek word is *chilia* and explains why belief in the millennium is sometimes known as chiliasm. It all comes from a passage in Revelation 20. The seer, John, sees in his vision an angel take hold of the devil and bind him with a chain in the bottomless pit for a period of one thousand years (verses 1–3). The souls of those who were beheaded for their testimony to Jesus are raised to life and reign with Christ for the thousand-year period (verse 4). At the end of the thousand years, or 'millennium', Satan is loosed from the pit, deceives the nations of the earth and then leads a combined demonic-human army against the 'camp of the saints and the beloved city' (Jerusalem). Fire, however, comes from heaven and consumes them, and the devil is finally cast out, never to return (verses 7–10).

The historical perspective
The notion of an idealized earthly kingdom of the Messiah before the eternal order is realized cannot find any direct support in the Old Testament. The fact that most of the Old Testament descriptions of God's future age of salvation are in this-worldly terms may, however, be seen as some kind of support for it. On the other hand, the vision of the future in Isaiah 65–66 of a

'new heavens and a new earth' was also influential in the later Old Testament and post-Old Testament periods, particularly where apocalyptic influences were also significant.

The idea of an earthly messianic kingdom was fairly widespread among Jews in the first century, though it was by no means universally held. It also appears in some early Christian writers. Justin Martyr, Papias and Irenaeus all held such a view. It was taken up by those known as the Montanists at the end of the second century after Christ, and was also held by a number of Anabaptists during the period of the Reformation. Other of the early fathers make no mention of it, so clearly it was never a universally held view. Augustine (4th–5th century) held this view as a younger man, but came in later life to believe that the millennium referred to the entire period between the two comings of Christ. The 'binding' of Satan during this period was to be understood in terms of the authority vested in the church to 'bind' and 'loose' sins – a reference to Matthew 16:19; 18:18 which the church at that time claimed to fulfil through the priesthood. The major reformers all rejected the idea of the millennium. Calvin for example held that it was 'too childish an idea to be even worth the bother of refuting'. The millennial kingdom of Christ was reasserted in the nineteenth century particularly as an integral element in dispensationalism (see below), and it is embraced by many Christians today, especially in the United States.

This historical survey is important in showing that there has been a variety of interpretations of this idea from the earliest centuries and no one view can claim to have been the only one. This should put us on our guard against interpreters who assert that their interpretation of the millennium is the only one possible for Bible-loving Christians.

There are three main interpretations of the millennium idea, though as we shall see even to state that is possibly oversimplifying the issue. We will explain each in turn noting their strong and weak points. I shall inevitably make clear which option I favour, and why; but I trust I will not be at all unfair to the views from which I must respectfully differ.

Post-millennialism

This position in general accepts the idea of a literal reign of Christ on the earth. Some, but not necessarily all post-millennialists view this as of one thousand years' duration. Others see the thousand years as only a symbolic reference. The point, however, which distinguishes post-millennialists from all others is that for them the return of Christ in glory will take place *after* a period of his reign on earth. This is expressed in the title *post*-millennialism; the prefix *post* is a Latin word meaning 'after'. The *parousia* will be after the millennium.

In general adherents to this view believe on the basis of passages such as Matthew 13:31–33, 47–48; 24:14; Mark 13:10; Romans 11:11–16; 1 Corinthians 15:25 that the work of the gospel will enter upon times of unparalleled blessing and fruitfulness through the whole earth, so that Christ's will is done and his rule established through the world before his return in glory.

It hardly needs saying that this interpretation of the millennium had many more defenders in the nineteenth century than it does today. The late nineteenth century was a time of tremendous progress and optimism in western European culture, and considerable progress was made during that period in the world-wide spread of the gospel; indeed the evangelization of the world seemed a possibility within a few decades. That bright optimism has subsequently been cruelly shattered by two world wars and all the massive problems which the world is faced with today. In face of the current general sense of crisis in human culture the post-millennial view appears to call for a greater faith in the progress of the gospel than most Christians feel able to commit themselves to without clearer and surer biblical testimony to support it. For, quite apart from the strangeness of its optimism in today's world, the post-millennial view also has to face some fairly searching biblical difficulties.

In the main it seems to run counter to the biblical teaching that the time prior to the return of Christ will be a time of persecution of the church when the fortunes of the gospel appear to be at a generally low ebb (Matthew 24:6–14; Luke 18:8; 21:22; 2 Thessalonians 2:3–12; 2 Timothy 3:1–7; Revelation 13). Something of the sharp edge of this difficulty is removed if we see these features as characterizing the whole of the period between the two comings of Christ rather than simply the final part just before Christ returns. However, even with this qualification one needs to admit that it is not easy to square these texts with a glorious millennial reign prior to the *parousia*. It is especially difficult to square such a view with the repeated warning of the Lord to be watchful in view of the unexpectedness of his coming (Matthew 24:42–44; etc.). Finally it runs into difficulty with the biblical teaching regarding the *present* reign of Christ. The early Christians believed that the resurrection and ascension of Jesus meant that he was now Lord and King in the universe (Acts 2:33–36; 3:13; 7:55–56; Ephesians 1:19–22; etc). Indeed Jesus claims such himself: all authority in heaven *and on earth has been given* to me (Matthew 28:18, my emphasis). And this reign of Christ is not without its evidences. The achievements of the church in history may be meagre by some standards, but they are not negligible in their testimony to the fact that Christ's reign is already begun. The tendency of the post-millennialists therefore to postpone that reign to some future period of blessing prior to the *parousia* appears to be incorrect in the light of both Scripture and experience.

There is one aspect of post-millennialism however which *is* worth retaining. That is its optimism concerning the work of the gospel. We are living at a time when the very fabric of life as we have known it for several generations appears threatened. Mankind faces today problems at a number of points which appear almost without precedent in their intensity and size. In this atmosphere of crisis it is not difficult to believe that we are living in the end times, particularly if we are persuaded that the Bible predicts times of great stress and unbelief immediately prior to the Lord's coming. As a result of these factors there is a mood of pessimism in some quarters as far as the prospects for the church are concerned. The Scripture says that the end times will be times of rejection of the gospel, so there is no real point in energetic witness or high evangelistic expectations. Against this pessimism the post-millennial view has something important to say. If the signs of the times are less clear than is commonly assumed, as we have sought to show in chapter four, and we do not have good biblical grounds for making the assumption that this is the final generation, then the door is obviously opened for a much more hopeful view of the possibilities before us. Full-blown post-millennialism may have been discredited, but if this is not the last age, or even if in general it is, may we not yet hope to see great fruitfulness from the preaching of the gospel throughout the world?

Pre-millennialism

The pre-millennialists share with the post-millennialists the view that we should anticipate a future, earthly reign of the Lord Jesus Christ. Most pre-millennialists regard the thousand years of Revelation 20 as meaning just that; some others take it as a symbolic figure for a definite period of time. The distinctive feature of the pre-millennial view lies in the relationship it conceives between the time of this earthly reign of Christ and the *parousia*. For pre-millennialists the thousand-year reign or its equivalent will take place after the second coming. The *parousia* is *before* (Latin = *pre*) the millennium.

The biblical support for this view is drawn from passages which describe the messianic kingdom in terms of an ideal earthly order (cf. Isaiah 2:2–5; Micah 4:1–3; Isaiah 11:1–10; 35:1–10; 65:17–25; Zechariah 14:9, 16–17; Psalms 45; 72; 110; 24:7–10). It also appeals to references which appear to present the coming age in material forms (Matthew 19:28; Acts 1:6–7; Mark 10:35–40; John 5:25–29; Revelation 5:9–10) or which it is claimed allow the idea of a passage of time between Christ's return and the eternal age (1 Corinthians 15:23–25; 1 Thessalonians 4:13ff.; Ephesians 2:7). The major support however is clearly Revelation 20:2–5. It is certainly doubtful whether this view would ever have been held on the basis of the other biblical passages cited had the passage in Revelation 20 not been present.

Actually Revelation 20 is not altogether clear about who exactly is involved in the millennial reign. At first reading it appears to concern only those who 'had been beheaded for their testimony to Jesus'. The following phrases 'who had not worshipped the beast ... and had not received its mark' may well simply be further descriptions of this particular group of martyrs. If this is correct then the idea of a literal millennial kingdom is confined to a tiny proportion of the saints of God and the pre-millennial scheme is seriously damaged. It has to be admitted that this is the most natural reading of the Greek; however, it is difficult to be absolutely dogmatic. The claim that the martyrs are in some way representative of the whole number of the saints or that succeeding phrases 'who had not worshipped the beast' etc. refer to other much larger groups cannot be absolutely ruled out either grammatically or even theologically, though it needs to be conceded that neither of these is the most natural reading of the text.

Another problem with Revelation 20 being referred to an earthly reign of Christ with his saints is that there is no indication that this reign is on the earth at all. The whole book of Revelation spends much of its time with realities 'behind the scenes' in the heavenly order (cf. 4:2; 11:19; 12:1ff.; 15:1ff.; 19:1ff. etc.). John refers to 'throne' no less than 47 times in his visions and with the exception of the throne of Satan (2:13) and the beast (13:2; 16:10) every other reference is to a location in heaven. Why then should chapter 20 be the single exception? Again this is not in itself a conclusive objection, but it is obviously disturbing to find difficulties of this magnitude arising from the passage upon which a whole view is based.

Similar questions arise with the other pre-millennial 'proof-texts'. 1 Corinthians 15:22–28 *can* be understood in a pre-millennial manner, but that is hardly the only or most obvious meaning of Paul's words, and it is significant that critics of pre-millennialism commonly cite this very passage – and also 1 Thessalonians 4, the other major pre-millennialist source – as supporting a synchronization of the great final events. The fact that the events which they place on either side of the millennium will in fact happen concurrently appears to be taught by passages such as Matthew 13:37–43, 47–50; 24:29–31; 25:31–46; John 5:25–29; Daniel 12:2; Acts 24:15; Revelation 20:11–15.

Underlying the pre-millennial interpretation of Revelation 20 and the Old Testament accounts of the coming messianic kingdom, there commonly lies a particular approach to biblical prophecy. This is the view that biblical prophecies should be interpreted literally rather than symbolically. Thus the pre-millennialists regularly accuse those who dismiss the millennial idea (see below on amillennialism) as being guilty of two errors.

1. The first error is inconsistency, in that they treat some prophecies literally (e.g. the fact that Christ is coming again) but others only symbolically (e.g. that there will be a millennial kingdom). The right to decide which is literal and which is symbolic lies apparently with the amillennialist interpreter. It is therefore a position which depends in the end upon the personal whim of the interpreter. By contrast pre-millennialists are consistently literal and are therefore controlled by the objective teaching of the Bible.

2. The other error is lack of faith, since (it is alleged) underlying the attempt to interpret these prophecies symbolically is an element of unbelief. The amillennialist (see below) is perhaps more affected than he realizes by the sceptical spirit of the age. He has lost faith in a God who is 'able to do far more abundantly than all that we ask or think' (Ephesians 3:20). His dismissing of the literal meaning of the biblical prophecies is therefore really a confession of his failure to stand by the word of God no matter what may be the climate of current philosophy or science.

The limits of literalism
The charge of inconsistency, however, appears unwarranted in the light of the following considerations.

1. All interpretations of prophecy and of apocalyptic are of

necessity non-literal at points. No one has ever been completely literal. Thus for example no pre-millennialist interpreter known to me has ever genuinely believed that at some point in the future a beast with precisely the features described in Revelation 13 will actually rise out of the Atlantic or some other ocean, or that the prophecy of Messiah's rule in Psalm 110:1 means that we are to anticipate the Messiah actually using his enemies as a foot-rest! Pre-millennialists in fact acknowledge this point by the way they use Old Testament prophecies. Thus the battle of Armageddon which it is claimed is described in Ezekiel 38 is not fought with cavalry but, of course, with tanks and nuclear weapons. But why *not* on horseback, since that is what the Bible actually says (Ezekiel 38:4)? So the truth is not that the prophecies are to be either literally or spiritually interpreted, but rather that we all have to decide what is literal and what is 'symbolic'. The subjective element is present for everyone.

2. When we study the way in which the Old Testament prophecies have already been fulfilled in the New Testament then the 'literal or symbolic' maxim really comes apart. The New Testament shows that there is no single rule of thumb which we can apply. Certainly some prophecies are fulfilled to the letter (one thinks here of the prophecies of the sufferings of Christ in Isaiah 53 or Psalm 22). Others, however, are seen as fulfilled 'spiritually' or even allegorically. Galatians 4:21–31 is a clear breach of the pre-millennial rule about interpreting prophecy. Passages such as Luke 4:18–21, Acts 15:13ff., Luke 1:32–33 also appear to breach the principle. These references are particularly to the point as in different ways they show that the prophecies of the 'material, earthly' kingdom of God in the Old Testament have found spiritual fulfilment in the experience of the church within the kingdom brought by Jesus.

3. Apocalyptic elements in books such as Daniel and Revelation obviously demand a symbolic interpretation. The use of symbol was of the nature of the apocalyptic method. What we need to do in order to interpret them correctly is to identify the symbols as sharply as we can and then interpret their usage on the assumption that the writer is writing in a consciously coded

form. To champion 'literalism' at this point is completely to misunderstand the nature of these writings.

In an earlier chapter we tried to identify the principles which should govern our handling of biblical prophecy. These principles will not solve all the problems overnight, of course; no method can. However, they are the basis for a method which is appropriate to the form of the prophetic writings and which fully honours the authority and divine inspiration of the Scriptures.

Is God able?

The second charge cannot be too lightly shrugged off, however. If we are not persuaded of the pre-millennial view, let us be quite clear that it is not on grounds of a too-easy capitulation to the mood of our times. Do we believe that God can in fact bring about the kind of thing which the millennial kingdom expresses? Are we prepared to take the Bible's teaching about the future victory of God really seriously and come to terms with what it means for life *in this world*, rather than pushing it all up into the sky in some rather vague talk about God's final victory 'one day'?

Before leaving this discussion of pre-millennialism there is a further important aspect which needs to be brought into the picture; for very many pre-millennialists hold to their view of the millennium as part of a much fuller system of biblical interpretation, known as dispensationalism.

Dispensationalism

The system of interpretation known as dispensationalism is of comparatively recent origin. Much of its inspiration stems from the writings of J. N. Darby, one of the founders of the Plymouth Brethren, and dates therefore from early to mid-nineteenth century. Its extensive influence upon evangelical thought, particularly in the first half of this century, has been largely due to its being incorporated into the footnotes of the Scofield Bible.

The essence of dispensationalism lies in its conviction that

God's dealings with the human race have been divided into a series of successive historical periods or dispensations. There are seven such, each representing a different test of man and each ending in judgement due to man's failure. The seven dispensations are: (1) paradise (life before the fall, Genesis 1–3); (2) human self-determination (the fall to the flood, Genesis 3–7); (3) human authority (the flood to the call of Abraham, Genesis 8–11); (4) the patriarchal promise to faith (call of Abraham to ministry of Moses, Genesis 12 – Exodus 19); (5) law (Moses to the coming of Christ, Exodus 19 to Malachi) (6) grace, or the church (first coming of Christ to his return, Matthew 1 – Revelation 19); (7) visible millennial kingdom (from return of the Lord to the final events of world perfecting, world judgement, etc, Revelation 20:2–15).

The final two, the dispensation of grace and the dispensation of the visible millennial kingdom are together the period of the accomplishment of salvation. Despite the fact that some are saved during the church age, and that the saints share in Christ's reign during the millennium, and that there is widespread conversion to Christ's rule during it, both these dispensations will end in failure, like the others before them. Man in general rejects the gospel during the church age and the millennium itself will culminate after the devil is released (Revelation 20:7ff.) in the greatest revolt against God in all history. Only after this is put down will the eternal age appear, the kingdom of God the Father (1 Corinthians 15:28).

The kingdom and the church

An important aspect of many expositions of dispensationalism is the role of the Jews. It is held that Jesus' coming was with a view to offering the kingdom of God to the Jews. This was to be an earthly kingdom for which the sermon on the mount was the basis. Only after this offer was rejected did Jesus turn to the Gentiles and introduce the idea of the church. The church is a different notion from the kingdom and is not predicted in the Old Testament. The whole period of grace between the two comings of Christ, during which the gospel is offered to the nations and the elect from both Jews and Gentiles are called to salvation, is really a vast parenthesis to the major theme in God's redemption. This theme is the kingdom of God, which the Jews rejected but which will come into realization at the millennium.

What will happen at the end?
Many dispensationalists see the events at the end of the period of grace occurring in two stages. First Christ will come in the air for his saints both living and dead, who will be caught up to meet him in the air (1 Thessalonians 4:13ff.; John 14:3; 1 Corinthians 15:51–52). This is the so-called rapture of the church. Some believe that this event will not be visible to non-Christians and so refer to it as the 'secret rapture'. This event will not be preceded by any specific signs in the world and so it can happen at any time. The only intimation of it which non-Christians will have is that Christians have disappeared. Then will ensue a period of seven years ('Jacob's week' cf. Daniel 9:24–27; Matthew 24:15ff.; Revelation 4–18) during which the Holy Spirit is also absent. The gospel of the kingdom will be preached throughout the world by those who become believers due to the church's disappearance. Jews will be particularly involved in this witness which will be very effective, especially among Jews. During this seven-year period (some say after three-and-a-half years) there will be unparalleled persecution of the people of God (Daniel 9:24–27; Jeremiah 30:7).

It needs to be added that dispensationalists divide on the question of who will suffer the tribulation. Many take the view expounded here that the church will be absent (called pre-tribulationism, because the rapture takes place *before* the tribulation). Some take the position that the church will be present for the first half of the seven year period of tribulation (mid-tribulationism). Others again oppose the idea of the secret rapture and hold that the church will be present throughout the tribulation (post-tribulationism).

At the end of this time the second stage of this return of Christ will take place. He will come again to the earth, this time 'with' not 'for' his saints. The nations will now be judged, antichrist destroyed, the martyrs from the recent period of tribulation raised up, Satan bound for a thousand years and the millennial kingdom established on earth, with its capital in Jerusalem. It will be a visible, historical kingdom with Christ ruling within Jerusalem. The temple will be rebuilt and sacrifices (of a memorial nature) again offered. There will be widespread prosperity, the desert will blossom and human life will be prolonged. The world will be quickly converted to Christ's lordship. After the millennium Satan will be released and the hordes of Gog and Magog march on Jerusalem. There they will be destroyed by fire which will come down from heaven. Satan will be finally cast out into the bottomless pit. All the unbelieving dead of all the ages will then be raised and passed under judgement at the great white throne, and the new heaven and earth will be established.

A critique of dispensationalism

What may we say concerning dispensationalism? First, on the positive side, there are some clear biblical elements within it. Christ's coming was indeed first to the Jews, and the apostles followed the same precedent and order in taking the gospel out into the world. The Jews are and will remain a special people, as we sought to show in the discussion earlier; although their relationship with God can only be on the same basis as that of Gentile believers, namely repentance and faith in Christ. Further, in their witness to the need for constant watchfulness concerning the Lord's return dispensationalists have given a timely challenge to the 'post-millennial' atmosphere of the period at the latter part of the nineteenth and the earlier part of the twentieth century. By their stress upon the Lord's return, they kept this hope alive and vibrant at a time when many were tempted for a variety of reasons to forget or neglect it. Further we can honour the deep commitment to Scripture in many dispensationalist teachers. Some of the great leaders of this movement were (and continue to be) men of profound spiritual learning who studied Scripture with an immense diligence, and in this respect they represent a standing rebuke to what is often in the present day a comparatively superficial and easygoing approach to biblical study.

Having made these points, however, an increasing number of biblical students (myself included) find the whole scheme of dispensationalism inadequate and even positively unhelpful, and so (with great respect to its proponents) beg to differ. There simply is not the space to enter into a full discussion, but we can enumerate the issues which need to be raised.

1. The divisions into the seven dispensations appear on examination quite arbitrary. They seriously undermine the essential unity of the biblical message and even appear to call into question the self-consistency of God.

2. The idea that Christ came essentially to set up an earthly kingdom among the Jews and then postponed it until the millennium because of their rejection is a basic misunderstanding of the nature of the kingdom of God and of Jesus' own concept of the kingship he had come to exercise.

3. The distinction between the kingdom and the church is correct; they are not the same. But the difference between them is very far from the difference which dispensationalism assumes. The associated thought of the church as a parenthesis in the purposes of God shows a basic failure to grasp the way in which the New Testament sees the church as the fulfilment of Old Testament prophetic hopes for the messianic salvation.

4. The continuing place for the Jews in God's purposes is not wrong, but it fails to take sufficient account of the many ways in which the church has assumed the promises made to Israel.

5. The view of God's purpose in the present age as simply the calling out of the elect from a largely unbelieving generation imparts to the whole concept of the Christian life and to the church and its mission a pessimism and a separateness from the world which is one of the most serious practical weaknesses of dispensationalism.

6. The complex web of events associated with the return of Christ is without adequate biblical foundation. The New Testa-

ment presents the Lord's return as a single though many-sided event.

7. The notion of a secret rapture is particularly poorly supported in Scripture.

8. The picture of the millennial kingdom with Christ reigning visibly from a throne in Jerusalem, while animal sacrifices are being offered again in a rebuilt temple nearby, is an astonishing and incredible idea. It appears deeply dishonouring to the Lord, as is the thought that even after his visible enthronement evil has still to attain its fullest embodiment. Underlying this error is a mistaken literalism in handling prophecy and apocalyptic which we commented on above.

9. One of the most disturbing aspects of this whole scheme is precisely that it is a scheme. As a result of this approach the warm person-centred religion of the Bible is overlaid by a theoretical, impersonal scheme of happenings and events. While very many dispensationalists are exceptions to the rule, one cannot but wonder at the effect of this kind of approach upon personal religion and personal attitudes.

Pre-millennialism: a concluding comment

The degree to which the dispensationalist elements are adopted by pre-millennialists varies from teacher to teacher. At one extreme are those who follow almost the entire dispensationalist scheme but for one element, for instance a rejection of the teaching that the church will not pass through the tribulation. Many pre-millennialists however would simply maintain the idea of the two stages of Christ's coming, the first accompanied by the resurrection of the saints of God, followed by the period of Christ's earthly millennial reign, and then the second stage accompanied by the general resurrection, the final overthrow of evil and the judgement before the eternal age is inaugurated. Indeed the possibilities extend right down to the simple conviction that Christ will appear in glory to bring history to an end, but that before the eternal age fully dawns there will be a period of his visible reign in a renewed earth in the midst of his resurrected and glorified people. This highly modified and not unattractive version is, however, some distance from much pre-millennialism.

We have seen reason to criticize the pre-millennialist scheme at a number of points: the doubtfulness of its interpretation of the crucial passage in Revelation 20; its unnecessarily complex understanding of the *parousia* and events associated with it; and its ambiguous interpretation of biblical prophecy. However, having made these criticisms, pre-millennialism in its witness to the realism of the Christian hope is surely reflecting something which we dare not give up. It was upon this earth that man was called to live to the glory of God. It was on this earth that man was tempted and fell to ruin. It was on this earth that God in his grace came to call man back from the far country and restore him to his eternal purpose for him. It was on this earth that Christ came and died and rose. There is surely something fundamentally sound in the vision which looks for the fulfilment of the promise and the full vindication of God's purpose *on this earth* as well as beyond it. As a symbol of that dream pre-millennialism is surely worthy of some defence, if not in its detail at least in its deepest instinct.

Amillennialism

This view is more straightforward than the other two in that it simply rejects the notion of a literal earthly reign of Christ whether lasting for a thousand years or some other such period, and whether before or after the *parousia*. The whole millennium idea is a symbol only and ought not to be taken with any degree of literalism. Because this position effectively dispenses with the millennium it is commonly known as *a*millennialism (Greek *a* = without). Its view of the second advent insists that the whole thing refers to one single, though many-sided event. There are no stages or dispensations with series of events and resurrections and kingdoms. When Christ returns it will be the decisive culmination of all things and the world as we presently know it will give place to the new heaven and earth of God's eternal order.

What then are we to make of the passage in Revelation 20? Amillennialism is divided at this point.

A. Position A is that we should follow Augustine and see the millennium as being a reference to the entire age of the church between the two comings of Christ. Thus the 'binding' of Satan in Revelation 20:2 is a reference to the work of the Lord Jesus Christ in his mighty and decisive victory over the devil and all the powers of evil in his life and ministry. Jesus is the strong man who has bound the devil, as he himself claimed (Matthew 12:22–29). The 'coming to life' of the saints (Revelation 20:4) is a reference then to the regeneration of the people of God, their coming to life in Christ from being dead in trespasses and sins (Ephesians 2:1–2). They are therefore described as now 'reigning in life' with Christ (Romans 5:17; Ephesians 1:3; 2:6) in the heavenly places.

However, it has to be admitted that the exegesis which this scheme offers of Revelation 20 is not altogether convincing. Apart from the difficulties mentioned earlier about only the martyrs apparently being involved in the millennial kingdom and the reign apparently being exercised in heaven rather than on earth, there is the further requirement that we differentiate between the 'coming to life' mentioned in verse 4 and the 'coming to life' in verse 5. The amillennial interpretation under review here requires us to interpret the first as a spiritual rebirth and the second as the general resurrection of the dead at the end of the age. But will this do? At this point the plea of pre-millennialists for consistency in interpreting prophecy needs to be heard.

This view also has to cope with the problem that the devil does seem alive and pretty well in the period of the church and *not*, as would seem from the Revelation 20 language, shut up in a sealed pit and unable to deceive the nations any more. Certainly Christ has won a decisive victory over the devil and all the powers of darkness. The evil one is mortally wounded. The ultimate outcome of the conflict with the powers of darkness is not at all in doubt. Further the church may, through the power of Christ working through faith and prayer, actually 'bind' the devil in human history so that the gospel can be preached and believed and the captives of the devil redeemed and set free.

All that is true, and gloriously so, but when all that is said, the description in 20:2–3 does not square very well with the realities of human history. Was the devil 'bound' at Auschwitz? Was he 'bound' during Stalin's purges in Russia? And these are only two of the most 'demonic' of innumerable examples from the long history of man's inhumanity to man. Is he 'bound' in territories where the gospel has been virtually obliterated, such as in north Africa in the sixth century or in parts of China in the twentieth? Obviously it is possible to maintain the exegesis of Revelation 20 in face of these difficulties, but it is impossible not to feel some anxiety about it.

B. The other form of amillennialism takes very seriously the apocalyptic element in the book of Revelation, and hence does not feel bound by the literal meaning of much of its imagery, but rather treats it as inspired symbolism. The book is an elaborate, and to our modern eyes rather weird and exotic vision which is intended to convey several quite simple and yet tremendously important truths about God and his purpose in human history (see the earlier discussion on the message of the book of Revelation).

By this view the symbols are not to be interpreted literally, particularly the numbers. The reference to a thousand years is, by this view, a symbol of the completeness of God's victory. The sacred number seven is added to the number of the holy trinity, three, which number has equally sacred associations, and then the total, ten, is cubed to a thousand. In numerical language no clearer expression of perfection is possible. The number 1,000 in fact occurs several times in Revelation. The case for treating the number literally is no greater in chapter 20 than at any other point. Indeed there is a good case for saying that if the number 1,000 in chapter 20 is to be interpreted literally it is arguably the only instance of a literal interpretation of a number in the entire book.

The message of Revelation 20 is simply that those who appear to have lost most in this world because of their loyalty to Christ, namely the martyrs, have in fact lost nothing, but gained the supreme blessings of the presence of Christ and a share in his rule. The evil one has no further power over them and the triumph of Christ and his saints is utterly assured at the end of the age.

On the negative side the great danger of the amillennial view is that it can take the inspired Scripture of the book of Revelation so symbolically that it does not really impinge upon historical reality in this world at all. The Christian hope then dissolves into a general conviction that 'everything will turn out all right in the end'. But Revelation has sharper and clearer and more precise things to say than that, and the Christian's hope must have a clear point of relationship to the present historical process. This very relationship is expressed in the language of the Bible, 'a new heaven and a new earth'. A new earth is central to the hope. We are taught to anticipate the resurrection of our bodies, not just the immortality of our souls. In other words there is a real and genuine continuity between life in this world now and the life of the new world to come. In so far as amillennialism fails to make that point clear and plain it is to be ruled inadequate. Pre-millennialism may be guilty of an excessive materialism and an unfortunate tendency to systematize the Christian hope, but its instinct to represent the hope in real terms is not wholly unsound. Amillennialism, while arguably the best interpretation of the biblical teaching on the millennium, needs to keep before it the vision of a real future hope which is in continuity with human earthly existence as well as being in discontinuity from it. Only thus can it really serve to clarify the terms in which we, with all God's people, anticipate the 'glorious hope' of the return of our Lord Jesus Christ.

One final comment needs to be made. Let us not get this millennial question out of proportion. Although it is not without importance as far as the full terms of the Christian hope are concerned, it is not the central concern as far as the Bible is concerned. To divide sharply from Christian brothers and sisters over this issue is therefore a major error – arguably worse than any errors in the millennial views themselves. The centre of the Christian hope, as I urged in chapter 2, is the Lord Jesus Christ himself and his glorious appearing. Millennial views are secondary to Christ. When we allow them to usurp Christ's place and make differences at this point a cause for breaking of fellowship with those who love Christ and revere the Scriptures as profoundly as ever we do, then we are guilty of needlessly dividing Christ's body and thereby dishonouring our blessed Lord. Let us keep the Bible's priority clear. The Christian hope is hope of *Christ*. To *him* be the glory for ever.

7

DEATH AND RESURRECTION

The Bible's teaching about the Last Things is many-sided. We have looked at the great central event, the return of Christ. We have looked at the way in which we may interpret that event in relation to the other aspects of the Christian hope. There remains, however, another group of truths and aspects most of which are concerned with life after the return of Christ, particularly as they affect the future of the individual, and to these we now turn. (For a fuller discussion of death, see one of the companion volumes to this in the Kingsway Bible Teaching Series.)

Death

'It is appointed for men to die once' (Hebrews 9:27). There can be very few statements in the entire Bible which are less likely to be challenged than that one. All men are mortal. Astonishingly, despite its obvious truth, this fact does not appear to register too clearly with many people. They spend much of life preparing and planning for things which in the end may never happen, but give comparatively little attention to preparing for death, which is an utter certainty.

The wages of sin
In speaking of death the Bible consistently links it to sin (cf. Genesis 2:17; 3:19; Psalm 90:7–11; Romans 1:32; 5:12, 16, 17; 6:23; 1 Corinthians 15:21; Galatians 3:13; James 1:15). Death

is not something natural to man. It has arisen because of man's rebellion against God and is a form of God's judgement upon us for our sin.

The Bible however has something else to say about death – it is not the end of man's existence. Death may be inevitable, but it is not terminal. Man is by nature an eternal being.

Is the soul immortal?

At this point we need to distinguish carefully between what the Bible teaches and another view with which it is frequently confused. This non-biblical view is referred to as 'the immortality of the soul'. It teaches that there is a part of us which is divine, a 'spark' of God within us. This is our soul. It is the bit of us which is immortal, i.e. which will survive death and enter heaven. By contrast with this the Bible's conception of the future of the Christian is 'the resurrection of the body'. What the Christian is to anticipate is life in the new resurrection body with which God is going to clothe his people (cf. 1 Corinthians 15:35–57) in the new heaven and earth which Christ will establish when he comes. The Christian hope is of the continuation, through the grace and power of God alone, of full embodied life in the new heavens and earth. It is therefore a hope of the 'resurrection of the body'.

Easter hope

When we believe in Christ and commit ourselves to him as Lord and Saviour, it is not just that our sins are forgiven; we are also united to Christ. Our lives are caught into a oneness with him. In particular we share in the death and resurrection of Christ. The events of the first Easter become events in *our* lives too. Thus Christians, almost incredibly, can testify with Paul 'I have been crucified with Christ' (Galatians 2:20) and I 'have been raised with Christ' (Colossians 3:1; cf. Romans 6:1ff; Ephesians 2:5–6; Philippians 2:5ff; Colossians 2:12; 2:20; 3:1ff; 2 Timothy 2:11). We have died in the death of Christ and risen in his resurrection. The Christian therefore has passed through an experience of world-transforming significance, the crisis of death and resurrection with Christ. He has been through the valley of death and emerged to new, eternal life.

Of course if Jesus delays his second coming the believer will face 'death' in the sense that he will pass from immediate space-time existence. But although his obituary notice may appear under the 'Deaths' column in the newspaper, in effect it will not be an announcement of death in the full and terrible sense, death as the judgement of sin. Rather the obituary notice concerns the believer's transfer from one level of eternal life to another. The essential person already united with Christ is already caught into the eternal life of the kingdom and moves forward irresistibly and incorruptibly through history on into the new heavens and earth which are the continuing shape of the order of the kingdom.

The *parousia* is therefore not the point at which 'everything has to be done' as far as the believer's entrance upon eternal life is concerned. Rather it simply brings to light and carries into full effect what was attained in essence in the death and resurrection of Christ. It was there at the first Easter that death was slain and its sting drawn. It is in the light of the cross and empty tomb of Jesus that we cry with Paul, 'O death, where is thy sting? O grave, where is thy victory?' (1 Corinthians 15:55, Authorized Version). In faith in Christ we enter *now* upon eternal life and look for the life of the new heavens and earth beyond the return of the Lord in the resurrection body which he will give us.

If the true Christian hope lies not in the immortality of the soul but in the embodied life of the new heaven and earth this raises obvious questions regarding the condition of the believer in the interval between his physical death and the *parousia* when he shares in the resurrection and the new order. This is the question of the intermediate state.

The intermediate state

Under this theme we encounter again that peculiar 'tension' between the 'now' and the 'not yet' which is of the essence of biblical faith. The Christ has come and wrought his finished work of redemption, but he has still to come in glory. The new age of the kingdom is present in the Holy Spirit, but it is yet to appear in its fullness. The Christian has died and passed to new, eternal life, yet he will still experience physical death and can only enter upon the full life of the kingdom beyond this life. If we accept this tension as part and parcel of the biblical witness then we are in a position to look biblically at the 'intermediate state'.

There is no problem here of course for those who believe in the 'immortality of the soul'. At death the essential person, the disembodied soul, lives on in the next life. The biblical hope, however, is of embodied existence corresponding to that which God has created and gives man in this world. In what sense then can the believing dead, or the unbelieving dead for that matter, be said to 'live' in the period between their physical death and the *parousia* and the resurrection in the future? What can be said from the Bible about the abode of the dead?

Five features

There are five things to be noted.

1. *Abnormal:* there is more than a hint in Old Testament teaching concerning life beyond the grave that it is less substantial than that experienced by us here and now. Paul reflects a little of the Old Testament sense in 2 Corinthians 5:4 where he speaks of being 'unclothed'. It is not the full Christian hope, though it is nonetheless preferable to life in the present.

2. *Non-temporal?:* one way out of the difficulty created by the thought of a disembodied existence is to argue that passing out of this life means passing out of the whole time order. Thus from the perspective of the experience of those who die, there is no break in time between death and the *parousia*. Their next conscious moment is the Lord's coming and the resurrection. It would be unwise to over-dogmatize concerning what the experience of time could mean beyond death. There certainly appears an incongruity in seeing it as virtually identical with

what we have known here. On the other hand, such biblical testimony as we have would point against such a solution.

3. *'Sleeping'*: one of the commonest biblical terms for the state of the dead is sleep. It is not difficult to see how the term could come to be used, since the dead commonly give the impression of taking repose, and death certainly implies some of the things which sleep implies; rest from labour, easing of responsibility, abstraction from immediate involvement in events, a different kind of awareness (Mark 5:39; John 11:11; Acts 7:60; 1 Corinthians 15:51; 1 Thessalonians 4:14). Some however go beyond the metaphorical to the literal and argue that the use of this term in Scripture implies that death induces a cessation of all consciousness until the *parousia* and resurrection.

However, this appears irreconcilable with scriptures referring to a conscious existence during the intervening period (see Luke 9:30; 23:43; Acts 7:55–56; Philippians 1:23; Luke 16:22ff.). If we reject the 'non-temporal' view then there would appear something of an incongruity in the death of Stephen, that he should be granted a vision of the Lord in his glory promptly to be debarred from a consciousness of that glory until the end of the age (cf. Acts 7:55–56). Philippians 1:23 'to depart and be with Christ' appears particularly to the point here (cf. also the sections in Revelation 5:13; 6:9–11; 7:9ff; 15:2ff; 19:1ff.).

4. *'With Christ'*: here is the most important description (cf. Luke 23:43; Revelation 6:9; Luke 16:22). To be 'away from the body' (2 Corinthians 5:8) is nonetheless to be 'at home with the Lord'. To die is to depart to be 'with him'. It is therefore, for all its limitations as compared with the fullness which awaits at the *parousia*, still preferable to all that we may know in this life. It is indeed 'far better' (Philippians 1:23).

5. *'Waiting'*: It is however not the full reality. Thus the Scripture depicts the martyrs beneath the altar of God as also waiting and anticipating the new age: 'How long, O Lord?' they cry (Revelation 6:9–10). The tension therefore which the church experiences, caught between the two ages, is a tension which exists also for the dead. For them too the great decisive victory

has been won by the Lord Jesus Christ in his death, resurrection and exaltation. For them too there is the longing and anticipation of the full implementation and manifestation of that triumph at the end. How time is experienced by the dead is something we cannot be sure of. That it is different is inherently probable, yet there do appear hints of an awareness of the passage of time.

Among the various mistaken and unbiblical notions which have gathered round the 'intermediate state', two in particular should be noted.

Purgatory

One notion is the Catholic idea of purgatory, the suggestion that in the period between death and the fullness of the new age the souls of believers are subjected to an experience of purification to fit them for the final vision of God.

There is no biblical evidence for such an idea. 1 Corinthians 3:15, which is often cited in this connection, concerns the judgement of the Christian's service and ministry, which will be tested by fire in the sense that all that is unworthy in it must be removed before it can be presented to the Lord. In the case of a careless and shoddy workman, virtually all he has attempted will be lost, though he himself will be saved, 'only as through fire', i.e. like a man escaping from a fire which consumes all his goods.

Other passages mentioned as supporting the notion of purgatory – Isaiah 4:4; Micah 7:8; Zechariah 9:11; Malachi 3:2,3; Matthew 12:32; 18:34 – certainly do not teach such a view by any straightforward exegesis. The clearest reference lies in a non-biblical book, 2 Maccabees 12:42–45, and even there we find an element which contradicts official Catholic teaching, the deliverance from purgatory of those committing mortal sin. We need have no hesitation in asserting that this erroneous teaching has no basis in the word of God.

A second chance

The other mistaken view is the idea of a 'second chance' during the intermediate state, which was taught from time to time by particular thinkers in the last century, and today is incorporated in some statements of universalism (see below). There is, however, no biblical foundation for such a view.

The resurrection

One of the major accompaniments of the *parousia* according to the New Testament will be the resurrection of the dead. All who have lived upon earth will share in this mighty act of renewal.

It is sometimes alleged that the Old Testament has no resurrection hope, but this is contradictory to the evidence. Significantly our Lord found testimony to resurrection in the Old Testament when debating with the Sadducees who denied it (Matthew 22:29–32). Other clear references to a resurrection hope in the Old Testament occur in passages speaking of eventual deliverance from the grave, Psalms 49:15; 73:24ff.; Proverbs 23:14; Job 19:25–27; Isaiah 26:19; Daniel 12:2 (Ezekiel 37:1–14). The resurrection of the dead is taught explicitly in the New Testament in Matthew 22:29–32;Mark 8:38; Luke 18:22; 12:33; 16:19–31; John 5:23–29; 6:39, 40, 44, 45; 11:24, 25; 14:3; 17:24. Other major passages are 1 Corinthians 15; 2 Corinthians 5:1–10; 1 Thessalonians 4:13–16; Revelation 20:13.

A bodily hope

The resurrection is the true goal of Christian redemption. We need to underline again that the goal is not in terms of the immortal soul; the true fulfilment of the work of Christ and the kingdom of God is not in the realm of disembodied spirits. In the biblical understanding the body also is from the Lord, and the body also is for the Lord. Further, all disease and physical deformity will flee before the Lord at his coming. He comes to restore all that has been corrupted, to raise man in the totality of his life to the fullness of his created glory.

What do we mean by the resurrection of the body? Clearly we can have no clear concept from our present limited experience, but we can, however, make two general points about it.

1. It will be a different level of existence from our present experience. It is life in the new heavens and earth. It will be an existence without the limitations brought about by the fall and sin. If we take the resurrection body of Jesus as a model we are immediately conscious of new and strange properties (John 20:19–29; Luke 24:31, 36; Acts 9:1–8; 1 Corinthians 15:5–8). We shall be changed (1 Corinthians 15:51). Flesh and blood as we know them here 'cannot inherit the kingdom of God' (verse 50). It will be different and new and transformed as the rich stalk and ear of grain is different from the bare, gnarled little seed from which it grows (verses 35–38).

2. The resurrection will retain some degree of continuity with the existence which we experience now. This is not due to any essential worth or attainment on our part, but solely to God's goodwill and sovereign mercy.

Some have expressed uncertainty about this teaching in face of the sheer magnitude of what is implied when one reflects upon the facts of physical dissolution and decomposition. Others have stumbled at the almost 'science-fictional' atmosphere of some presentations of the truth of the resurrection. As far as the magnitude of the task is concerned we do well to ponder the words of Jesus to sceptical hearts in his own day, 'You are wrong, because you know neither the scriptures nor the power of God' (Matthew 22:29). If we recall the doctrine of creation *ex nihilo*, the fact that all that now exists in the universe was brought into being out of nothing by God's power, we are surely delivered from any thoughts of the 'difficulty' of the resurrection for an omnipotent God. As far as the fictional, fantastic atmosphere is concerned, we do well to ask ourselves whether we have not harboured unbiblical notions of 'spiritual immortality' and whether the real stumbling block in our minds is our preference for a salvation which embraces only the soul rather than the whole man. If we still find problems then we need to return to the great central reality, the resurrection of Jesus Christ, and hear again his word and call, that 'where I am you may be also' (John 14:3).

8

JUDGEMENT

When speaking of the resurrection and the life of man after death the Bible does not only speak of a resurrection to life, it also speaks of a resurrection to judgement (John 5:29). Accordingly any exposition of the Bible's teaching on the Last Things needs to give serious attention to the theme of judgement.

In the Old Testament God often appears as the 'God of judgement' (Malachi 2:17; cf. Deuteronomy 1:17; Isaiah 30:18; Psalm 97:2; Micah 6:1–2; etc.), or as the 'judge of all the earth' (Genesis 18:25). This does not imply that God simply stands back from the human scene and acts as the universal umpire weighing up good and evil. Rather, the thought is of God taking vigorous action against evil. God's judgement is his mercy and wrath working themselves out in human history and experience (Deuteronomy 10:18; Psalm 25:9; Isaiah 4:4; Jeremiah 1:10; Ezekiel 23:11; etc.). As the Old Testament draws to its close the thought of the judgement of God becomes more and more bound up with the coming 'Day of the Lord' which will accompany the coming of his kingdom (Amos 5:18ff.; Obadiah 15; Zephaniah 1:14ff.; Malachi 4:1ff; etc.).

The New Testament in developing the theme continues the thought of God's judgement as belonging to his nature and being part of his essential activity (1 Peter 1:17; Romans 1:18; Hebrews 12:23; Revelation 16:5ff.). God's judgement is not confined to the future but is already at work in human life (Romans 1:18, 22, 24, 26, 28; John 8:50; Revelation 18:8). It is particularly associated with Christ, who exercises the Father's judgements (Matthew 3:11–12; John 3:19; 5:30; 8:12; etc.). In the New

Testament however the spotlight falls upon the 'judgement to come', a future and final judgement which will be one of the accompaniments of the return of Christ (Matthew 25:31–46; John 5:22, 27ff.; 1 Corinthians 4:3–5; Romans 3:5ff.; Hebrews 6:1–2). This is the coming Day of judgement (John 6:39; Romans 2:16; 1 Corinthians 5:5; 1:8; Ephesians 4:30; Philippians 2:16; 2 Thessalonians 1:10; 1 Peter 2:12; 2 Peter 2:9; 3:7; 3:12; Jude 6; 1 John 4:17; Revelation 6:17; 16:14). Christ himself will judge (John 5:22; 12:47–48; Acts 10:42; 17:31; 2 Timothy 4:8). All men will be judged; none will be absent (2 Timothy 4:1; 1 Peter 1:5; Hebrews 12:23; Revelation 20:12ff.). Even the angels will be passed under judgement (2 Peter 2:4; Jude 6). Every aspect of life will come into account, including the 'secrets of men' (Romans 2:16), 'the counsels of the hearts' (1 Corinthians 4:5, Authorized Version; cf. Mark 4:22; Luke 12:2–3), and 'every careless word' (Matthew 12:36). The judgement will not be confined to unbelievers. Christians too will face judgement (Matthew 25:14–30; Luke 19:12–26; 1 Corinthians 3:12–15; 2 Corinthians 5:10; Hebrews 10:30; James 3:1; 1 Peter 1:17). There can be no avoiding this coming judgement (Hebrews 9:27); it is as certain as death (Hebrews 10:27; Romans 2:3). Nowhere is this fact more clearly asserted than in the parables of Jesus (Matthew 13:24–30, 36–43, 47–50; 21:33–41; 22:1–14; 25:1–13, 31–46; etc.).

The basis of judgement

The basis of judgement will be man's response to the revealed will of God. It will therefore include the entire range of human experience, thoughts, words and deeds, and will be such as to allow account to be taken of different degrees of knowledge of God's will, and hence of different degrees of ability to fulfil it (Matthew 11:21–24; Romans 2:12–16). It will be utterly just and completely convincing (Genesis 18:25; Romans 3:19). The judge of all the earth will do right, and every mouth will be stopped in acknowledgement of the justice of his judgements (cf. Job

40:1–5; 42:1–6). Like Job we can cling to the justice of God (Job 13:13ff.; 16:18ff.; 19:23ff.; 23:1–17; 31:1–40). In the face of the frequent injustices of life in the present age we can rest in the certainty that God knows all, and that he is not mocked, and that he has appointed a day in which he will judge the world in righteousness (Acts 17:31). We can trust him to act in his future work of judgement with the same perfection and triumph which he manifests in the present in his works of grace and sovereignty.

Faith or works?

Sometimes a difficulty is alleged as far as the basis of judgement is concerned, in that Scripture appears at points to speak with two voices. On the one hand our justification before God is said to rest on faith alone apart from our good works (Romans 5:1–2; 3:28), and yet judgement is elsewhere declared to be on the basis of human works (Matthew 16:27; 25:31–46; Romans 2:6; 1 Corinthians 3:8; Revelation 22:12). The difficulty is more apparent than real. The following points need to be borne in mind.

1. One of the great words used in the New Testament for Christian salvation is justification (Romans 5:1; 8:30; Luke 18:14; Galatians 2:16; 1 Corinthians 6:11; etc.). It is a legal term and means that the Christian is acquitted at God's judgement seat. In other words it claims precisely to anticipate the final judgement and it affirms that the man or woman who is trusting in the perfect merit and finished work of Christ is guaranteed acquittal at the day of judgement (1 Corinthians 1:30; Romans 5:1; 8:1). Thus the New Testament teaching on the nature of salvation has built into it the assurance that the danger of final judgement and condemnation has passed for ever. Faith in Christ means that Christ's perfect obedience in life and death is imputed to us here and now and will stand to our account on the judgement day. Putting this another way, Christ's 'good works' are made ours, and so we need have no fear of judgement to come if we are trusting in him. The biblical references

which link judgement to our human 'works' cannot therefore be interpreted in a way which calls this fundamental truth into question.

2. Our relationship to the perfect character and works of Christ is not merely that of their being 'put to our account' in an external way. Faith means being united to Christ in such a manner that our life becomes bound up with his (Romans 6:1ff.; Galatians 2:20; Ephesians 2:5ff.; Colossians 2:20; 3:1–2). As a result of this there will inevitably be some moral change in our lives. We cannot be bound up with Christ without something of his righteous character being expressed in us. This is the insistence of James (cf. James 2:18ff.). Faith without works is dead because there is no such thing as a faith in Christ which does not bring us into union with him, and that includes union with him in his death and resurrection with all the shattering implications of that for our moral character. We can put this point in a rather more technical way by saying that if justification does not lead to sanctification (the process of becoming holy) then it is shown to have been no justification at all (cf. Hebrews 2:10ff,; 1 John 3:5ff.; Romans 6:1ff.).

This does not mean of course that the Christian does not sin; far from it. Indeed it is the common testimony of Christians that it is only after conversion that they begin to see sin for the terrible thing it is, and it is only then that they begin to discover how deeply sin is entrenched in their personalities. Yet, alongside that, the Christian *is* being changed, slowly, but nonetheless surely 'from one degree of glory to another' (2 Corinthians 3:18).

The implication of all this for the question of the basis of judgement lies in the fact that the Christian's life will bear certain evidences of his having become Christian. There will be certain 'works' which will be evidence of that faith. These 'works' are the direct fruit of being united with Christ by the Holy Spirit. They do not represent virtuous human attainments on our part which could become the basis for our acquittal before God. They are part of God's gift to us in Christ, but they are nonetheless real. The Christian then in this rather special sense can be said to be justified by 'works' because these 'works' of God in us are evidence of our faith in Christ.

3. When Jesus was once asked by would-be disciples, 'What must we do, to be doing the works of God?' he replied, 'This is the work of God, that you believe in him whom he has sent' (John 6:28–29). To believe in Christ is the supreme 'work' which God requires of us. Thus in this further sense it is again seen to be true that the Christian is justified by 'works', the very unique and special work of exercising faith in Christ.

4. One New Testament passage has proved particularly difficult to reconcile with the insistence that justification is by faith in Christ alone; the parable of the sheep and the goats in Matthew 25:31–46. On the basis of this parable all kinds of claims have been made.

Some have asserted that it teaches that people can be 'anonymous Christians'. These do not believe in Christ in any personal way, indeed their minds may explicitly deny him, yet because of various forms of 'good works' such as helping the needy, feeding the hungry, even fighting wars of liberation, they will be acquitted at the judgement because they have in these 'good works' unwittingly ministered to Christ himself.

This interpretation of the parable, however, suffers from one fatal weakness. It requires us to interpret this single passage in a way which is clearly not in harmony with either the rest of Jesus' teaching or the Scriptures as a whole. On the other hand, if there is a way of interpreting this passage which would bring it into clear harmony with other aspects of Jesus' teaching, then that approach ought to be followed. And it can be so interpreted. Jesus states in the parable that the 'good works' which the 'righteous' perform are done to his 'brethren' (Matthew 25:40). They are acts of mercy towards the disciples of Jesus. Now Jesus elsewhere refers to the identification of himself with his followers as being so close that people's response to his followers becomes their response to him (Matthew 12:48–50; 10:9–14; John 20:21ff.; Matthew 10:40; 18:18; Mark 9:37). Thus 'he who receives you receives me'. Hence the acts of compassion exercised towards Jesus' disciples are evidence of a true response to Christ himself. Jesus' reference, therefore, is to specifically Christian works in which a person's faith and commitment to Christ and his cause is declared.

In interpreting the parable in this way we do not of course wish to deny the fact that many non-Christians do perform 'good works' and sometimes such as to put Christians to shame. But these 'works', even when carried to the limits of self-sacrifice, are not able to acquit people before God's judgement seat. These very people too are fallen sinners who at many points in their lives have disobeyed God and are resisting his claims upon them. The only hope for them, as for the Christian, is Christ: 'there is salvation in no one else, for there is no other name under heaven given among men by which we must be saved' (Acts 4:12).

In these ways the Bible's teaching about the basis of the coming judgement can be harmonized. It speaks with one voice in this matter. The basis of judgement will be our response to God's will which is made known to us in our conscience and supremely in his word, written in Scripture and incarnate in his Son. Since we are all sinners and have disobeyed God's will for us, the only hope of acquittal lies in casting ourselves on God's mercy in Christ. Justification is by faith in Christ alone.

Unbelief and judgement

There is one further view of the basis of judgement which requires comment. This is the notion that the *only* basis upon which a man or woman may be exposed to the final judgement and condemnation of God is their explicit rejection of the gospel of Christ. In support of this Scriptures such as John 3:18, 36; Mark 16:15–16; Romans 10:9–12; Ephesians 4:18; 2 Peter 2:3ff.; 1 John 4:3 are cited which represent unbelief as the ground of condemnation.

Three points can be made in answer to this.

1. These passages only prove that faith in Christ is the one way of salvation, which is not the same as proving that conscious rejection of Christ is the only ground of condemnation. No

doubt unbelief is a great and serious matter and the form in which sin expresses itself when men spurn the one hope of their redemption, but it is not the only form of man's revolt against God, and hence it is certainly not the only possible ground on which man stands condemned before God.

2. In fact the Bible represents men as already under condemnation before the gospel is preached to them, and it is precisely this prior condemnation which represents the need of men to which the gospel comes as God's gracious answer. The effect of the gospel is not first to create and second to remove man's condemnation, but to deal with the condemnation which already hangs over man's head (cf. Romans 1:18; 2:12; 5:16, 18; Ephesians 2:4–5; 5:3–6; Colossians 3:5ff.).

3. The view that the gospel creates the possibility of man's condemnation as well as of his deliverance cannot but have a most debilitating effect upon evangelistic and missionary zeal. If it were only by rejecting the gospel men were finally condemned and if, as statistics show, the majority of those who hear the gospel do not accept it, then on purely utilitarian grounds it is in the interests of the greatest happiness of the greatest number not to preach the gospel at all, and indeed to do all in our power to stop its being preached. This ludicrous and patently unbiblical conclusion shows how mistaken is the original premiss.

Those who haven't heard the gospel

The germ of truth in this position is that increased knowledge and increased opportunity do imply increased responsibility. Scripture certainly does recognize that men are not equal as far as their opportunity to know God is concerned, and this factor will be taken into account when God exercises his judgement (Matthew 11:20–24; Romans 2:1–24; 2 Peter 2:21). The principle of Luke 12:48 'to whom much is given, of him will much be required' is applicable at this point. Thus the general comment that those who have never heard the gospel will be judged by the light they have is correct. However, God has not left himself without a witness to any man (Acts 14:17).

He has made himself known to all men through the world around them which he has made (Romans 1:19–32) and more particularly through his moral law which all men have some awareness of through their conscience (Romans 2:14–16). God's 'word' which comes to men by these means is not as clear or full as that which comes through the gospel and the written Scriptures. It is nonetheless not insignificant and is of sufficient clarity to render all men inexcusable for their rebellion against God and their disobedience to his will as it has been made known to them.

Hence we must conclude with the Bible that all men have turned away from the light of God, whatever form that light assumed in their particular case, and hence that 'all have sinned' and come under condemnation (Romans 3:9–23). Only in Jesus Christ is there hope of salvation (John 14:6; Acts 4:12; Ephesians 2:12).

Hell

The Bible teaches clearly that there will be a division at the final judgement between those who are variously described as the righteous and the wicked, or the elect and the non-elect, or those whose names were found written in the book of life and those whose were not (Daniel 12:1–3; Malachi 3:18; Matthew 13:30; 39–43; 13:49ff.; 25:32ff., 41, 46; Mark 13:27; John 5:28–29; 1 Corinthians 1:18ff.; 2 Corinthians 2:15–16; Revelation 20:11–15).

A biblical reality

The common biblical word for the fate of those who pass under God's judgement is hell. The terrible idea of eternal punishment is reflected clearly in a number of texts, Matthew 5:29–30; 10:28; Mark 9:43, 45, 47; Luke 12:5; James 3:6; etc. Other plain New Testament references to the fate of the unjustified are in 1 Peter 3:19; 2 Peter 2:4; Romans 1:18ff.; 2 Corinthians 2:15–16; Ephesians 2:3; Philippians 3:19; 2 Thessalonians 1:7–10; 1 Thessalonians 5:3; 2 Thessalonians 2:10; Revelation 20:14–15.

The Bible's teaching here is quite unambiguous and of awesome seriousness. Those who remain unrepentant when confronted by God's claim upon them, who reject his will when it is made known to them, and who continue through their lives in the blasphemy and rebellion which sin implies, will face a fearful judgement.

No doubt some of the language used to describe hell is symbolic, just as is the language used to describe heaven. Pictures are obviously all we have to describe realities which lie beyond our present experience. However, the fact that we are thrown back on symbols does not mean we can disregard them. These pictures are not the fruit of a merely human imagination. They are God-given, God-inspired pictures. They cannot tell us everything, but they will not mislead us.

There can be no evading the Bible's witness at this point. Hell is a reality, and a reality of almost unspeakable solemnity. If we were to select one biblical description in particular it would be a phrase from 2 Thessalonians 1:9– 'exclusion from the presence of the Lord'. The unjustified are shut out from God. Hell means the permanent inaccessibility of God. It is the carrying through into eternity of the decisions taken by men in this life, the confirmation in the eternal order of a judgement already passed (John 3:18ff.).

A correct reserve

Obviously we need to use a genuine reserve in speaking of hell. The attempts made in earlier generations to dwell at length on the details of this future state of judgement in order to drive people into the kingdom of God were surely misplaced.

However, in using reserve we ought nonetheless to be guided by Jesus and the Bible in the degree to which that reserve operates. Jesus at times saw the need to speak with great starkness concerning the coming judgement if people continued to resist God's claims upon them. If we call Jesus 'Lord' of our lives then he must be Lord also at the point of our understanding of the gospel and the way we expound it (John 13:13). It simply will not do to claim a loyalty to Jesus and yet be prepared to set aside what was by any reckoning a very significant element of his teaching. On what grounds do we claim to submit to the teaching of Jesus about compassion and faith and reject his equally plain teaching about holiness and judgement? In this sense the question of judgement is a good test of how biblical our religion is. Is it a faith which rests ultimately in the word and promise of God? Or is it in the end determined by our own preferences and experience?

We need to beware, however, of attempting to take the final judgement of God into our own hands and to start apportioning people to hell or heaven. God retains judgement to himself. He will determine every man's destiny. Indeed there is more than a hint in the Bible that there are going to be some surprises on the judgement day (Matthew 7:21–23; 25:37; 25:44; 21:31; etc.). We can be assured that on that day the mercy of God will reach as far as divine mercy can reach. If we are truly trusting in Christ then we need have no fear as far as we ourselves are concerned. For the rest we can leave matters in the hands of God. But in doing so we cannot be indifferent to the plain teaching of Scripture: 'God is not mocked, for whatever a man sows, that he will also reap' (Galatians 6:7), and 'it is a fearful thing to fall into the hands of the living God' (Hebrews 10:31).

Universalism

This is the view that in the end all men and women will be saved. Although in this life many do in fact reject the gospel when it is presented to them, and infinitely more who never hear the gospel do not live up to the light of God's will which comes to them through their conscience, nevertheless at the end all will be brought into God's eternal kingdom.

In support of this view it is urged that God's mercy is of such extent and the merit of Christ's sacrifice is of so great a value that all will be forgiven and enter the new heaven and earth prepared for the people of God. Sometimes biblical passages are cited in support, in particular Romans 5:12ff.; 2 Corinthians 5:19; Ephesians 1:10; 1 Corinthians 15:51; Philippians 2:10 1 Timothy 2:4; 4:10. Universalism is in fact very widespread in the church today. But is it true? Obviously no one ought to find delight in proving it wrong. There is something in the universalist view which accords with the longing of any sensitive person, particularly if they have had close acquaintance with the complexities of human experience, the pressures of environment upon behaviour and the confusions and half-suppressed yearnings for goodness of even wicked men. However, in the end these things cannot override the plain teaching of Scripture, nor can they be allowed to distract us from estimating sin and its judgement in the light of what it all means to God.

As far as biblical teaching is concerned universalism simply will not do. It is abundantly clear that the distinction between Christian and non-Christian, between those who have responded to God's grace in Christ and those who have spurned it, is a radical one in this life, and will continue to be a radical one after death (cf. 2 Corinthians 5:17; 2:15–16; 1 Corinthians 1:18, 24; Acts 2:38ff.; 10:43; 13:38; 16:30–31; 1 Corinthians 6:11; 1 John 3:14; John 3:36; Ephesians 2:1–5; etc.).

None of the texts which universalists cite will really make their case when closely examined. Two factors need to be kept in view. The first is that when the Scripture speaks of all men acknowledging Christ as Lord at the end of the age that does not mean that all will do so freely. Obviously Christian believers will rejoice to bow the knee to him at his coming. The ungodly however will do so in anguish (cf. Revelation 1:7). No doctrine of universalism can be built on the fact that Christ is destined to be revealed as Lord over all at his coming.

The second factor is that the gospel was preached in the first century against a background of groups who tried to confine salvation to those who belonged to their particular racial group (the Jews) or to those who were initiated into their peculiar rites (the gnostics). Against these exclusive groups the Christian gospel stands out in its universal appeal. Here is salvation for *all* who will believe in Christ. Racial background, intelligence quotient, social background and supremely moral attainment or the lack of it are all irrelevant. 'Whosoever will may come' (cf. Revelation 22:17).

It is these factors which explain the seemingly universalist reference in most of the texts which are cited in support of that position, and it is perfectly clear that Paul, from whose letters almost all of these texts are culled, was not a universalist (cf. Ephesians 2:3; 5:4–6; 1 Corinthians 1:18–24; 9:22; 11:32; Philippians 1:28; 3:18–19). Paul gloried in the universal offer of the gospel. It was a message with power to save even the worst and most unworthy. No matter what a man or woman had been they could come to salvation. But when Paul came on to the question of how that salvation could be appropriated then he is undeviating in his insistence that sinners must personally trust themselves to what God has done in Christ.

Jesus is equally difficult to interpret in universalist terms. His parables of judgement are especially clear on the fact that not all men will be saved (cf. Matthew 13:37–43, 49–50; 22:11–14; 25:40–46; Mark 12:9; etc.).

Further, as we noted previously, the final judgement will be before God. There in his holy presence sin will be seen for all that it means to God. We for our part tend on the whole to take sin fairly lightly. We are certainly quick to find mitigating circumstances to excuse misdemeanour, and the current social sciences give us plenty of ammunition for this if we want it. God, however, cannot take sin lightly. It is part of that resistance to his lordship which has risen up against him in the universe and which contradicts his loving purposes and strikes at his glory. He cannot ignore it and remain God.

Just how serious a reality sin is can be seen at Calvary. There we see what sin does to God and what God must undergo to pardon it. Sin is no trifle. God cannot tolerate it; he must execute his judgements upon it. If therefore men and women choose to cling to it even in face of God's love for them in Christ then they must face the fearful consequences of falling under his judgement themselves.

God is holy. He has eternally separated himself from sin. He therefore cannot receive sinners unless they come to him on the basis of the merit of Christ in and upon whom God has poured out his holy wrath against human sinning. Sin must be judged in a moral universe such as ours. If we do not accept the judgement passed upon sin in Christ and his cross then we must face it ourselves on the judgement day.

All this makes clear that what is at stake in the struggle with universalism is not just the interpretation of certain biblical passages but the very nature of God. Universalism requires us not only to revise our view of judgement, but also to change our view of the Judge.

Conditional immortality

This view teaches that the unjustified will simply pass into oblivion either at death or at Christ's judgement seat. Man was not created immortal; rather immortality is a gift of God in Christ to all those who believe in him. By their rejection of the gospel unbelievers forfeit their opportunity of receiving immortality.

Obviously this doctrine is an attempt to avoid the error of universalism and yet at the same time take some account of the genuine moral problem of a literally eternal judgement.

It also claims to have some biblical support: (1) 1 Timothy 6:16 which, it is claimed, teaches that only God is inherently immortal; (2) in Scripture immortality is ascribed only to those who have believed in Christ; (3) biblical terminology ('destruction', 'death', 'perish') is alleged to support it, and also references such as 1 Corinthians 15:51, which should be rendered: 'we shall all sleep [i.e. all will die] but not all will be changed [i.e. only believers will be raised to life in the new age].'

Against this, however, are the following points.

1. The immortality of man is certainly derived from the fact that he is God's creature, so it is correct to say that immortality belongs inherently only to God. But that is not quite the same as saying only God is immortal. Further, since unbelievers are also made in God's image, most interpreters have

seen that as implying that man is an immortal being by virtue
of being God's creature in this special sense (cf. Genesis 1:27;
2:7). Such an implication is certainly present in the New Testament when Jesus is spoken of as *the* image of God (cf. 1
Corinthians 15:49; 2 Corinthians 4:4; Colossians 1:15).

2. When the Bible speaks of the immortality of believers it does
not refer to mere continuation of existence but to that 'eternal
life' which is the life of God in the new age of the kingdom
of God. The alternative to having this is not that of ceasing
to exist, it is living in the old age of sin. Thus unbelievers alive
at the present moment do not have 'eternal life', i.e. they are not
in the kingdom of God, but they are certainly alive. There is
no evidence that this distinction will not continue to operate
after physical death.

3. The Bible uses a variety of terms to refer to the judgement
of the impenitent. Certainly one or two of these might be
construed as pointing to the annihilation of the unjustified, but
others clearly cannot, and the proposed rendering of 1 Corinthians 15:51 is clearly forced.

Whatever attraction this position might be thought to hold
at other points it appears impossible to square with the Bible's
teaching. The continued existence of the unrighteous after death
is taught in Ecclesiastes 12:7; Matthew 13:49–50; 25:46; Romans
2:12.

There is in addition the penal aspect of final judgement.
Sinners will receive then the just deserts of their sin. They will
be the objects of the divine retribution. Hell belongs, as we
have seen, to the moral vocabulary of the Bible. Annihilation,
however humane it might appear on some accounts, would on
others deny this moral-retributive element, since one can hardly
speak of the operation of the divine justice of God in the case
of a man who passes away to oblivion after a life of gross self
indulgence and evil. Does it square with the biblical witness to
the justice of God that a Hitler has passed into oblivion and
will therefore never be called to render account for his enormous
wickedness?

In all this we must not forget that we see 'through a glass, darkly' (1 Corinthians 13:12, Authorized Version) and that symbolism is certainly a factor in the biblical teaching, nor can there be any doubt that the thought of *eternal* judgement is an awesome one even for the most depraved. However, the terms of Scripture as we have them do clearly tell against conditional immortality.

The results of judgement

God's judgement will mean the banishing of evil in all its forms. The devil and all the hosts of wickedness will be routed and submitted to final destruction and judgement (Revelation 20: 7–10; 2 Thessalonians 2:8). Sin will be put away and with it all those things which it brings in its train: disease, pain, tears and sorrow (Revelation 21:4; 1 Corinthians 15:26; Isaiah 25:6–9). The very created order will also be delivered from the cycle of decay (Romans 8:19–21; Isaiah 35; etc.). In his final judgement God himself will be vindicated in his triumph over all his enemies (Revelation 19:1–3).

9

HEAVEN

The ultimate goal of the people of God and the reality towards which all God's purposes are moving is the new state of things which the Bible calls heaven. The return of Christ will bring this present world as we know and experience it to an end. The *parousia* will in turn set in motion the final events, the resurrection of the dead and the judgement of all men. Some interpreters would wish to interpose a millennial reign of Christ, as we saw in chapter six. In our discussion there we expressed our serious reservations about this view, but even if we allow for some such interlude we shall eventually enter upon the new heavenly world which will be the abiding home of the people of God. Before beginning an exposition of the biblical teaching about heaven, there is another aspect to take into account, the notion of rewards.

Rewards

This theme could just as readily have been discussed under earlier sections, which dealt with the judgement of the people of God, but because people often link it in their minds with the thought of heaven, as when they refer to 'heavenly rewards', it seemed appropriate to deal with the subject in this chapter.

We are concerned here with passages of Scripture which speak of God's people receiving, in the heavenly age, certain returns for their work and service in this world in the shape of 'rewards' (cf. Matthew 5:12; 6:1–6, 21; 10:41; Mark 9:41; Luke 6:23; 2 John 8; Revelation 11:18). The last reference, in Revelation, perhaps puts the matter more clearly than any of the other references. Here the climax of history is asserted to be 'the time for the dead to be judged' and also for 'rewarding thy servants'.

Jesus and the apostles lived and taught within a religious tradition (Judaism) where the idea of future rewards for faithfulness, and also conversely punishment for unfaithfulness, was a commonplace. Jesus in particular sought to correct the way in which this teaching was understood. This is the force of the passage in the sermon on the mount dealing with piety (Matthew 6:1–6). The Pharisees, in accordance with the assumptions of the Judaism of their day, took the view that God would reward acts of piety and self-denial regardless of the motives which prompted them. Jesus devastatingly exposes the hypocrisy of such a view and its openness to misuse through human vanity and self-esteem. The rewards of God will be for those who practise their piety with no concern to attain human praise, but who rather perform it all humbly and shunning public acclaim. Jesus therefore sets the whole doctrine of rewards on a new footing altogether, but he does not thereby reject the basic underlying conviction that there will be heavenly rewards and punishments relative to our lives and service in this age. It therefore appears at other points in his teaching, as we have seen in the earlier references.

What are we to make of this? Two comments need to be made.

1. One or two of the biblical passages imply that the matter of rewards is not confined to the next life but that the principle of rewards and punishments is already in operation (Exodus 20:5–6; Psalm 37:5–6; Proverbs 13:13; 19:29; 25:21–22). This note is probably more clearly sounded in the Old Testament where there is on the whole less clarity about the future life and the rewards and punishments of the future age, but it is present in the New Testament too, as we noted above. The principle of rewards here and now is true in the general sense that the man of faith will frequently experience greater happiness, personal fulfilment and sense of security and peace of

mind than his unbelieving neighbour. It is true also in the sense that the man or woman of faith has the incomparable privilege of knowing God in Christ and all that that involves. The fellowship of God's people is commonly another enrichment and 'reward' which the non-Christian cannot experience on a comparable level. Equally the man or woman who rejects God and his truth will most frequently experience a loss of fulfilment and happiness and may fall prey to some moral weakness with all the attendant sorrow and regret. This latter (of course) is only a general comparison. One could cite exceptions either way, but there is sufficient truth in it to warrant the comment.

2. As far as heavenly rewards are concerned, two New Testament passages are particularly pertinent. The first we referred to above, 1 Corinthians 3:10–15. Here the relative value of a Christian's service is likened to the relative durability of various building materials, wood, hay, stubble, gold, silver, precious stones. There will be some kind of assessment made in the future, at 'the Day' (verse 13), which must mean the Day of the Lord, the *parousia* and the coming of the eternal age. The service of each will be tested 'by fire' and only that which endures this test will remain for the eternal age. However, if a man's work survives this test 'he will receive a reward' (verse 14). We are not told what the reward will consist of, but we may fairly infer that the value will be relative to the degree of durability of the work he has done.

The other passage is the parable of Jesus in Luke 19:11–26. Care needs to be exercised here since parables in general are presented to make one central point and we dare not over-press the details. In this case the servants' work is again brought under scrutiny and those whose work is attested receive relative rewards. The distinctions in the rewards are different degrees of responsibility after the king has returned.

It is impossible to speak here with certainty. What we can assert however is that our stewardship of talents, gifts, opportunities, ministry, witness, service and the like will be subject to some kind of assessment before the Lord at his coming, and that in so far as we have proved 'good and faithful' servants we will receive an appropriate 'reward' in terms of the satisfaction of seeing our work preserved for the eternal kingdom, and perhaps also in terms of additional degrees of responsibility in the heavenly age.

The life of heaven

Anyone looking for a detailed description of the life of the people of God in the heavenly age is going to be disappointed. Heaven by definition is that which we do not have now. It is true that we have the Holy Spirit and that, as we have seen earlier, one of the ways in which the New Testament understands the Spirit is as the 'fore-taste' or first-instalment of the life of heaven (cf. Ephesians 1:13–14; 2 Corinthians 1:22; 5:5; Romans 8:16–17). Thus the life of heaven is not something concerning which we have no knowledge whatsoever. However, even though we have received something of the life of the heavenly age in the Spirit, we remain in the body of death confined by the limitations of this present fallen order. We can only see 'through a glass, darkly'. The distinction between what we know 'now' and what we shall know 'then' (1 Corinthians 13:12) cannot be overcome.

However, we are not completely in the dark. Some light does shine through to us in the inspired Scriptures and from them we can venture certain assertions concerning the destiny which awaits the children of God.

1. It will be an *embodied life*. Thus the prospect is not of a heaven of pure spirit. The 'new earth' will obviously be very different from 'the form of this world [which] is passing away' (1 Corinthians 7:31), and indeed 'heaven and earth', as we have known them, '*will* pass away' according to Jesus (Matthew 24:35). Nevertheless the present creation waits with us in hope of sharing in the coming glorious liberty of God's children (Romans 8:19–25) and so there must be some degree of continuity between the old earth and the new. On the personal human level, although we ourselves must eventually go down

into the dust of death if the Lord delays his coming, yet our flesh will also rest in hope (Psalm 16:8ff.; Acts 2:26; Job 19:26). We shall rise from the dust of death clothed in the new immortal resurrection bodies which God shall give us (1 Corinthians 15:35-57).

We therefore anticipate a heavenly life in which our self-conscious, embodied existence will be continued, though obviously at a new level and with many new and enhanced powers.

2. It will be a *social life*. It is surely of significance that all the Bible's pictures of the life of heaven are corporate. It is presented again and again in social terms (Isaiah 2:2ff.; Daniel 7:13-14; Zechariah 14:5; Matthew 24:31; 8:11-12; Ephesians 5:27; 1 Thessalonians 4:16ff.). The images vary. It is seen as a perfect city (Isaiah 2:2ff.; Philippians 3:20; Hebrews 11:10; 13:14; Revelation 21-22), as a victorious kingdom (1 Corinthians 15:23ff.; Philippians 3:20; Hebrews 12:28), as a holy temple (Ezekiel 40-48) and as a wedding feast (Matthew 8:11-12; 22:1-14; Luke 14:16-24; Ephesians 5:27; Revelation 19:7).

The common element in all these images is the fact that we shall be together with all the people of God. Just as salvation here and now is a matter of being gathered out of isolation into the body of Christ and being made one with all God's regenerate people, so that corporate dimension is destined to endure through the resurrection into the state of glory. There we will be one people of God, and indeed one of the perfections of heaven will be precisely the perfection of relationships with all God's other children.

The life to come is therefore wrongly conceived when it is presented as a personal, lonely pilgrimage to some exalted vision of God. It is rather the fulfilment of all God's purposes for his creatures, not least a fulfilment in mutual relationships. When God stated concerning unfallen Adam that it was 'not good' that he be alone, he indicated plainly that a significant dimension of human fulfilment lies in man's relationships to his fellow creatures. Heaven therefore will hold out to us un-dreamed of possibilities at the level of our social relationships.

If so many of life's 'solid joys and lasting pleasures' here and now are mediated to us through our human partners and neighbours, how much more will that become so in the heavenly society.

3. It will be a *responsible life*. The biblical basis of this assertion is less clear than that of earlier or later ones, but there is at least a suggestion at one or two points that the life of heaven will involve continuing and remarkable new responsibilities. Revelation 22:3 tells us that 'his servants shall worship him'. This clearly implies a continuing relationship of servant-Master as far as the Lord and his people are concerned, and servants without 'service' would surely be unthinkable.

The Greek word for 'worship' in the latter part of the phrase in Revelation 22:3 is in fact closely allied to the thought of service. Now of course the worship which we shall offer in heaven will itself be a service rendered to God, but there may be other forms of service as well. The parable in Luke 19:11–26 certainly carries the thought of responsibility in this life being carried over into the new age, and Paul in 1 Corinthians 6:2–3 speaks of saints as destined to judge the world and the angelic hosts.

God's purposes of salvation on this earth are in some way central for his purposes in the whole universe (Ephesians 3:10). It would be no flight of imagination, therefore, to picture the saints as destined for a role of great significance in the coming ages as God's great unfathomable purposes roll on into the mists of eternity and gather under them worlds and kingdoms yet unborn. Who can guess what heights we are destined to tread in the service of our God in the coming ages?

4. It will be a *God-centred life*. Here we arrive at the supreme feature of the life of heaven; all else we may say about it is secondary to and arises out of this. The manifestation of God himself, the sense of being as never before in his presence is the thing which will characterize the new life above and beyond everything else. Scripture refers to this as the vision of God, 'they shall see his face' (Revelation 22:4; cf. Matthew 5:8; Hebrews 12:14), 'we shall see him as he is' (1 John 3:2).

There is of course a sense in which we cannot ever 'see' God fully, for his majesty and deity are such that no creature could be exposed to it and live (cf. Exodus 33:20; 1 Timothy 6:16), and that will remain true for the life of heaven. In his grace and condescension however he veils himself so that we can approach him (Exodus 33:21ff.; Isaiah 6:5), as he did pre-eminently in the incarnation (John 1:18).

We may be assured that this principle will continue to apply in the new age. He will manifest to us such of his glory as we can receive and we may be confident that that will be such as can never be captured in language or expressed in speech. 'We shall see him' in his triune fullness, our glorious God who is Lord over all, blessed for ever. Like the psalmist we 'shall be satisfied with beholding thy form' (Psalm 17:15). To see and know God, to know just as we are known (1 Corinthians 13:12), is the essence of the heavenly life and the fount and source of all its bliss: 'in thy presence there is fullness of joy, in thy right hand are pleasures for evermore' (Psalm 16:11). Therefore, we may be confident that the crowning wonder of our experience in the heavenly realm will be the endless exploration of that unutterable beauty, majesty, love, holiness, power, joy and grace which is God himself.

5. It will be a *perfect life*. In the new age man will attain to the fullness of life for which he was originally destined. Man will find a perfection of relationship with God, with his neighbour, with his environment and with himself. Man will perfectly glorify his maker and find full self-fulfilment. All that has spoiled the attaining of these divinely intended ends in this life will be removed, sin, temptation, weakness and the rest, and man will be free again, as the ruler of the world and vice-regent of God, to attain the heights of moral and spiritual grandeur for which he was originally intended in the divine purpose (Genesis 1:28; Psalm 8:4–6).

6. It will be an *endless life*. It would show a foolish insensitivity to the change in the conditions of existence with the coming of the new age to suggest that the time sequence will remain un-altered. We cannot possibly grasp what time may mean in the

heavenly world. Hence speculations about the dangers of boredom are irrelevant, as indeed they are irreverent, when we recall that the heart of the experience of glory will be the exploration of God himself. All we can say with respect to the time element is that Scripture speaks of the limitlessness of time. We shall know a boundlessness and lack of confinement and constraint at the point of our prospects and anticipation which will reflect the boundlessness of the eternal God himself. What an 'eternal' existence may be like we can have little conception now, but we believe that in so referring to it we do not misrepresent it, and for the remainder we can rest in the love and boundlessness of God.

From God's perspective

To speak of the life of heaven in these terms, however, is to approach it from a secondary perspective. We have attempted to expound, within the limits which are inevitably imposed upon us, the life of heaven as it will be for the people of God. The deepest significance of the future glory, however, lies not in its meaning for man but in its meaning for God.

From this perspective the crucial factors are somewhat different. Of course by virtue of the love of God as creator and redeemer it is precisely the vindication of God which also produces the happiness of man. We are not therefore faced with alternatives. Yet we may note a relative order of significance. Above all things – heaven, the glory of the new heaven and earth, the fullness of the kingdom which is coming – are the final vindication and triumph of God. His glory, love and holiness will be declared and affirmed finally and for all ages against all that stands against him and against every denial of his being and work. In this sense there is an indissoluble bond between Last Things and First Things. Appropriately therefore Scripture begins and ends with a garden and a tree of life (Genesis 2:8ff.; Revelation 22:2ff.). God the creator is vindicated in his creation, and the purpose of God for man is affirmed anew. The creature who turned away from his creator is restored

to him and bows again in loving homage, and God is glorified.
Thus the authentic cry of heaven is the doxology

> Worthy art thou, our Lord and God, to receive glory and honour
> and power, for thou didst create all things, and by thy will they
> existed and were created [Revelation 4:11].

> Worthy is the Lamb who was slain, to receive power and wealth
> and wisdom and might and honour and glory and blessing! [Revelation 5:12.]

Then 'God will be all in all', and for this reason above all we
cry out from the heart with all the church in every generation,
'Even so, come Lord Jesus!'

10

THE CRUCIAL FACTOR

This chapter is so called because it is about something the Bible puts right at the centre and which Christians have frequently neglected in discussions about the Last Things. What is this crucial factor? It is the application of the truths of the Last Things to our lives here and now.

The application of truth

Application is not optional as far as biblical truth in general is concerned. If it is not applied it is not really true for us. God's truth cannot be had 'on approval'. He speaks to the obedient.

Thus 'crystal ball gazers' who spend much of their energies reading the signs of the times and plotting the blueprints for Armageddon and counting the heads of the beast from the sea (Revelation 13), but find no time to urge their hearers or readers to live lives of holiness or to commit themselves to evangelism or social renewal, stand self-condemned. The very Bible which they appeal to with such ingenuity to support their speculations passes judgement upon them.

An ancient tradition

People of this sort, whether they call themselves prophets or teachers or diviners of the times, are actually members of a very long tradition which stretches back across the centuries to the very beginnings of human society. Since the fall man has always been conscious of his frailty and transience. He is limited, dependent and exposed to all kinds of threats to his existence from forces such as disease, natural disasters, wars, famines, plagues, storms and so on. This insecurity is expressed in the fact of his unknown future. In that unknown dimension all these threats lurk and lie in ambush. Man knows the past, and though it may haunt him with its memories it cannot rise up and destroy him, or at least not directly. The present, elusive as it is, is nonetheless also man's possession. In the present he wills to carry out his plans and realize his desires. But the future is different. It moves ahead of man, always out of reach, always beyond his efforts to secure himself.

If only man could know what lies ahead ... if only he could secure himself against these dark threats which lie in wait for him. Who can tell him? In his search he turns to the medicine man, the diviner, the prophet, the guru, the fortune-teller, the horoscope writer, the astrologer. Every society has such figures, and no society can altogether dispense with them, for they meet such a deep-seated need in the human psyche.

The Bible is different

There are two major differences between all of these figures and the inspired writers of Holy Scripture who set forth teaching concerning the things which are yet to be. The first is that the biblical writers are part of the whole unique, divine revelation in Holy Scripture. What they convey is not the suppressed longings and fears of men, but the authoritative thoughts and words of God. Their prophecies belong to the history of salvation which lies at the centre of the Bible and which has its focus in the life, death and resurrection of Christ. It is the future as illuminated and interpreted by the coming and victory of God in Jesus Christ which they report and record.

The second major difference is the one we have noted already in this chapter, that their teaching about the future is thoroughly moral in character. It is teaching which is applied to the way we are to live here and now. It does not simply feed our curiosity or still our fears, but summons us to commitment, sacrifice and obedience.

If we indulge in speculations about the future using biblical materials, but do not clearly link our teaching to the history of salvation in Jesus Christ on the one hand, or to the clear biblical demand for practical moral application on the other, then for all our apparently biblical, orthodox and Christian approach, we stand in some respects alongside the medicine man and the fortune-teller rather than within the ranks of the God-sent messengers of the word of God.

The current danger

The danger of being misled at this point is always most acute at times of world crisis such as our own, when there is something of an apocalyptic atmosphere in society, and where this kind of 'speculative' teaching can command a wide and eager audience. After all, who wouldn't express interest in the future of the Soviet Union in its designs for world-domination? Who wouldn't be fascinated by the identity of the antichrist? Who wouldn't be attracted by the grisly details of the judgements of God poured out in history? It is precisely this deep human craving which is exploited so widely by the various sects who peddle their wares around our doors. Yet if we approach this whole area merely in a speculative frame of mind, without establishing a vital link to the history of salvation, and without a deep and conscious concern for the practical application of these truths to our lives and the lives of all God's people, we stand exposed to the possibility of becoming false prophets ourselves who serve the fallen cravings of the human heart rather than the Holy Word and truth of the living God.

What then *are* the moral implications of the doctrine of the Last Things? We may identify nine: hope, comfort, holiness, action, prayer, watchfulness, love, joy and praise.

Hope

The truths which we have examined in this book are the content of the Christian's hope for the future. In Titus 2:13 Paul refers to the Lord's return as 'our blessed hope'. In other words the truths of the Last Things should make the Christian into a person with hope.

The loss of hope

This is highly relevant at the present time, as increasingly we live in an age of hopelessness. The problems which face the human race today are vast and complex: shortage of food and resources combined with an unparalleled population explosion; pollution of the environment, rendering it unable to support human life; and in the longer term the destruction of the solar system as we know it. Alongside these 'natural' threats there are the ever-threatening menaces of the stockpiling of nuclear and chemical armaments, the great divisions of the races, the economic divisions between the 'haves' and 'have nots' and the ideological confrontation between east and west.

The cumulative effect of these problems has been to bring about deep uncertainty concerning mankind's ability to survive into the foreseeable future. One of the most sobering aspects of this mood of pessimism is that it is expressed perhaps more sharply in those who know most about the human situation. In other words this pessimism cannot be shrugged off as the outpourings of fanatics and misery-mongers. Our wisest men are today among our most anxious. Hope is in short supply.

Something of this loss of hope is seen in the way in which people live so much for the present moment. 'Live now, pay later' is the maxim for so many lives. The gods which offer immediate returns, the instant gods such as pleasure, sport, entertainment, sex, consumer products, expensive holidays, are the ones at whose shrines the worshippers throng.

In this age of hopelessness where the future is filled with uncertainty and threat, the Christian stands apart. His hope does not arise from an optimistic view of human nature like the humanist, or because like the Marxist he believes that man can be essentially changed by the alteration of the social context of his life. The Christian has hope because he believes in God, and in particular in a God who has created the world for a purpose. Although it may appear at times that God's purpose has been temporarily thwarted, it must triumph. Triumphed it has and triumph it will in Jesus Christ. The future therefore is bright with Christian hope, the hope of the return of the Lord Jesus in glory and of the new heaven and earth which God will establish at his coming. This world is not running amok, out of control and destined for disaster; God is Lord of his world and he will not permit it to escape from his grasp. Thus amid the pessimism and despair of men and nations, in face of the gloom and hopelessness of our age, the Christian remains at peace and can hold up his head in confidence and expectation. The Lord is coming – 'blessed hope' indeed!

Comfort

A second implication of the Last Things for the Christian is allied to the first: it is a source of comfort. This is Paul's concern in 1 Thessalonians 4. Some of the Christians at Thessalonica had become disturbed by the death of loved ones who had 'fallen asleep' (1 Thessalonians 4:13). They were sorrowing for them in a way which was indistinguishable from the sorrow of the hopeless pagans around them (verse 13). Paul shows that the Christian's convictions about the coming of the Lord have implications for our attitude to death here and now. We are not to 'grieve as others do who have no hope' (verse 13). The dead and we who are alive face together a future in which 'we shall always be with the Lord' (verse 17). Our destiny, whether we die before the Lord returns or are among those alive on earth at the time of his coming, is to 'live with him' (5:10), and hence we should 'encourage one another' (verse 11). The truths of the Last Things are therefore a comfort to Christians in that they strengthen their faith and encourage them in a new way to cope with the fact of death and all it implies in the breaking of even the dearest relationships.

The prospect of life beyond the grave also affects our personal attitudes. It teaches us that we do not need to grasp at life and try to force from it every vestige of fulfilment and satisfaction. The Christian also finds here a 'strength' to cope with failure.

Of course, the Christian can never be careless of moral issues such as his service and obedience to Christ, a point we will make again shortly, but when failure occurs, even devastating failure, the Christian again need not and must not finally despair. God's purpose for him is not limited to this life, and it is not going to be frustrated in the end even by his moral frailty. God will perfect his people.

This does not mean that our sin is of no consequence. The cross of Christ is the unanswerable argument against sin ever being treated with less than its true seriousness, yet even in our bitterest regrets and under the sharpest lash of our conscience we can find here the strength to repent, to find the mercy and forgiveness of our God and to crawl back on to the highway and set out once more towards the holy city.

In ways such as these the doctrine of the Last Things may be seen as a profound source of comfort and strength to the people of God.

Holiness

The third implication of the doctrine of the Last Things is holy living on the part of God's people. The fact of the coming of the Lord and all it will imply is a great summons to a life of energetic obedience to all the will of God spelled out in the teaching of Scripture and embodied for us in the person and ministry of Jesus Christ.

There are three lines of argument which lead from the fact of the Last Things to our moral character in the present.

This passing world

The first is that the coming end of all things shows us what an essentially impermanent and transient reality this present world is. We see therefore the folly of living for this world as though its life and its rewards were the supreme reality. In fact they are insubstantial and fleeting.

This is the point made in several of the New Testament passages on the Last Things. In 2 Peter 3 the apostle refers to the coming dissolution of the heavens and the earth (verse 10) and then continues: 'Since all these things are thus to be dissolved, what sort of persons ought you to be in lives of holiness and godliness!' In face of the transience of this earthly scene the Christian is called to embody the values which abide beyond its limits. He is called to distinguish between the passing and the permanent, and to make that distinction clear in his own personal choices and in the goals and values of his living.

Paul argues in a similar manner in 2 Corinthians 4:16–5:5. Thus what now appears as loss is seen to be everlasting and imperishable gain, and what now appears as earthly folly becomes a heavenly and eternal wisdom.

In the light of eternity and the coming victory of God all present standards and judgements are reversed. The earthly perspectives are overturned. To live for the things of this present age becomes the deepest folly. To live for the realities of the kingdom of God becomes the highest wisdom. The Christian then is called to put away an 'earthly' mind (Philippians 3:19) and to recognize that his true point of origin is 'in heaven, and from it we await a Saviour, the Lord Jesus Christ' (verse 20) (cf. also Hebrews 11:3, 7, 10, 13, 16, etc.).

Now we need to be careful lest this 'strangers and pilgrims' attitude should lead to a wrong kind of world denial. I shall try to show below that there is a genuine sense in which the Christian *should* be committed to the world, and indeed the Last Things constitutes a major biblical argument in support of this. However, at this point we need to reckon with a denial of the world in terms of its allurements and its honours, its acclaim and its prizes. This does not deny that Christians will be the objects of the world's honours at times, and indeed be called to exercise great human and 'worldly' responsibilities, but when such things do come the way of the Christian he should receive them with open eyes. He should recognize the transience of all such honours and the supremacy of the kingdom of God over all earthly and human orders and kingdoms. In the light of the coming dissolution of all things in earth and heaven he is the one who sets his heart on the things which remain.

A holy eternity

Secondly, the doctrine of the Last Things has moral implications in its declaration that the goal of the Christian and the church is a holy, righteous goal. The Christian is one who is destined for a holy eternity, and that fact has the profoundest implications for the way he lives here and now. We are called to move in the direction of our destiny and that means living now in a growing obedience to, and an increasing conformity with the will of God in Holy Scripture.

Various New Testament texts line up behind this principle. 2 Peter 3 for example buttresses the appeal to the passing nature of the world as a ground for holy living, with a reminder that the new heavens and earth which will replace the present ones will be those 'in which righteousness dwells' (2 Peter 3:13). The apostle John, referring to the New Jerusalem, says, 'nothing unclean shall enter it, nor anyone who practises abomination or falsehood' (Revelation 21:27). Everyone who 'loves and practises falsehood' is left outside the city (22:15). In contrast with all other concepts of the life to come, whether mystical or aesthetic, or belonging to other religious traditions, the biblical concept of the life to come remains profoundly and fundamentally moral. It will be a holy life, in a holy world. That is not all that we can say about it, but all that we say about it which omits this element is essentially different from the biblical picture.

This same point is put in another way when the New Testament refers to our destiny in terms of our being made in Christ's image (cf. Romans 8:28–30; 1 Corinthians 15:49). 'We shall be like him,' as John puts it (1 John 3:2), and therefore 'every one who thus hopes in him purifies himself as he is pure' (verse 3). Putting the same truth corporately, the church is destined to be made a fit bride for her heavenly bridegroom (Revelation 21:1–4). This will take place through the loving and sanctifying ministry of the Lord himself, so that 'he might present the church to himself in splendour, without spot or wrinkle or any such thing, that she might be holy and without blemish' (Ephesians 5:27; cf. Hebrews 12:1ff.; 12:14; 1 Thessalonians 2:12; 4:7).

We must give account

Thirdly, the doctrine of the Last Things summons us to holiness by virtue of the fact that his coming will expose us for what we are. This point is made in several places with reference to the actual moment of the Lord's appearing. In 2 Peter 3, Peter urges us to live lives of holiness and godliness so that we may be 'found by him without spot or blemish, and at peace' (verse 14). This appears something of an echo of Jesus' teaching in Matthew 24 about the need to 'be ready' for his coming and he likens himself there to a returning master of a household who will by his coming expose whatever his servants were doing at that moment (24:45–51). Clearly if the Lord at his coming finds us engaged in matters which are unworthy it will be a cause of considerable embarrassment to us, at the very least.

Peter's reference to being found 'at peace' is particularly apposite. The reference here is almost certainly to our being 'at peace' with others. In other words, our relationships with our fellows, whether inside or outside the church, ought to be in such order that they are fit to be examined by the Lord at his coming. For his appearing will effectively close our moral 'books' and be the prelude to his investigation of the state of our moral 'accounts'. In other words the return of the Lord will involve his judgement of our lives.

We have already covered the biblical teaching which justifies this statement (see above in chapter 8). Obviously this is a major reason for holy living. We must render account to our Lord (2 Corinthians 5:10; 1 Peter 1:17; etc.). Every man's work must be manifest (1 Corinthians 3:13); it will be exposed to the holy, purging fire of the Lord at his coming. Only that which is wrought out in the precious stones and gold and silver of sincerity, truth and concern for God's honour and the good of our fellows can hope to endure.

If we are those who truly believe in and anticipate the Lord's coming, then it will be evident in our lives. We will be those who 'strive for holiness' (Hebrews 12:14).

Action

The notion that belief in the Last Things and the return of the Lord leads to opting out of responsibility and to sitting around in holy huddles waiting for the rapture gets no encouragement whatever from the Bible.

One of the clearest statements of the return of Christ in the New Testament, Acts 1:11, occurs in the context of Jesus sending the apostles out on their mission to the world (Acts 1:8). In Matthew 24:45ff., in his parable of the returning master, Jesus implies that when the master comes he expects to find his servants busy in his service. It is the servant who neglects these duties and turns to self-indulgence who receives the master's wrath.

Paul had to deal with this very attitude of withdrawal in the light of the Lord's coming when he wrote to the Thessalonians. He has no time for it whatever. The idle are to be 'admonished' (1 Thessalonians 5:14), and when that counsel has not produced the necessary response he takes a stronger line in the second letter. Such believers are to be ostracized until they come to their senses: 'keep away from any brother who is living in idleness' (2 Thessalonians 3:6). Indeed, they should even employ the drastic principle, 'if any one will not work, let him not eat' (3:10).

The reason for this uncompromising rejection of any attempt to use the fact of the Lord's return as an excuse for laziness and inactivity is that such an attitude fundamentally misunderstands this whole area of doctrine. It denies rather than demonstrates its truth. The truths of the Last Things should lead to *activity*, not ease.

Three particular forms of activity flow from the biblical teaching on the Last Things.

1. Spread the gospel: The link between the end of the age and the spread of the gospel is established by Jesus in his Olivet discourse. Before the Lord's coming 'this gospel of the kingdom will be preached throughout the whole world, as a testimony to all nations; and then the end will come' (Matthew 24:14; cf. Mark 13:10). The universal spread of the gospel is identified by Jesus as one of the 'signs of the times', an indication of the imminence of the end.

Why precisely should the fact of the end lead to action in the form of spreading the gospel?

The warning note
One answer which is commonly given is that the end of the age will bring the wrath of God upon those who do not repent and believe in the gospel (cf. 2 Thessalonians 1:8). In view of this impending doom we ought to warn people and encourage them to turn to Christ so that they can escape the coming judgement.

If we think that it is always wrong to use fear to motivate people, we should remember that Scripture does sometimes appeal to men and women on the basis of the serious implications of unbelief and disobedience. In Genesis 2:17 God's prohibition of the fruit of the tree of the knowledge of good and evil is buttressed by a clear warning concerning the solemn implications of disobedience 'in the day that you eat of it you shall die' (Genesis 2:17). Another Old Testament example is Moses' farewell address to Israel in Deuteronomy (Deuteronomy 28:1–68). The message of Jonah is a particularly good example of this in the prophetic writings, 'Yet forty days, and Nineveh shall be overthrown!' (Jonah 3:4). In the light of this impending judgement the citizens repented and found God's gracious mercy and pardon (3:6–10).

John the Baptist made a similar appeal (Matthew 3:7–12). Nor did Jesus altogether disavow this. In Luke 13 he uses the disasters which have recently struck in the land, a Roman massacre and the collapse of a tower killing eighteen bystanders, to warn his audience, 'unless you repent you will all likewise perish' (Luke 13:1–5). (Cf. 2 Corinthians 5:11; Acts 20:20, 26–27, 31; Colossians 1:28.)

In the light of this and similar biblical evidence one cannot but wonder if the reason why such a warning note has so largely dropped out of preaching in our day is less a conviction that it is unbiblical as an indication of the capitulation of the church to the pressures of the world. It is perhaps in its way an indication of a loss of nerve, rather than a gain in understanding.

Will you be left?

Fear in itself however is not the truest motive for salvation. This also needs saying because of one particular way in which the fear element is appealed to when establishing the link between evangelism and the Last Things. This is the case with those who believe in a secret rapture of the church (see above in chapter 6). Since, according to this teaching, the people of God may be removed to be with the Lord at any moment, then how important to be numbered among them lest we be left behind when they have gone! This appeal has special force when applied to children who are faced with the prospect of their parents being taken away and they left behind. While God may have used this appeal in certain cases to awaken a concern for salvation, that does not imply that it ought to be either encouraged or used. The secret rapture idea lacks a clear biblical basis as we saw earlier. When Jesus did engage in evangelism he *nowhere* used this argument, except in the general sense that he warned his hearers that at the judgement there will be a separation of the sons of the kingdom from the sons of perdition (cf. Matthew 13:24–30, 36–43). Matthew 24:40ff. is not a counter-argument, for Jesus in this passage is *not* engaging in evangelism; he is informing the disciples concerning events associated with his coming.

This particular way of formulating the evangelistic appeal in the light of the Last Things is surely unworthy, particularly when addressed to children. It appeals to their deep emotional attachment to their parents and plays upon their vulnerability and dependence. Many have been driven right away from the kingdom by a deep abhorrence of a religion which could play on human feelings in this manner.

'The fullness of the Gentiles'

The link between the message of the Last Things and our

evangelistic witness is most clearly made at another point altogether which arises directly from the reference in Jesus' discourse (Matthew 24:14).

While the message of salvation in the Old Testament centres on God's dealings with Israel, God's underlying purpose was always to reach out through Israel to the world (cf. Genesis 12:3; Psalm 86:9; Isaiah 49:6; etc.). It was in these terms that Jesus formulated his great commission (Acts 1:8; Matthew 28:19–20). The earliest apostles and their Jewish converts found this universal dimension difficult to accept. Indeed there is evidence in the Acts of the Apostles of the Lord in the end having to use the persecution which arose over Stephen to drive them out of Jerusalem and into the Gentile world in fulfilment of his purposes for them. The story of Peter's experience at the house of Cornelius (Acts 10) shows how Peter overcame his Jewish prejudices and was brought to see God's purpose in terms of the whole world. This realization is focused in a phrase used by the Jews, who witnessed the conversion of Cornelius and his Gentile household, 'Then to the Gentiles also God has granted repentance unto life' (Acts 11:18). The whole issue was brought into the open at the Council of Jerusalem in Acts 15. Here James expressed the biblical vision, 'God first visited the Gentiles, to take out of them a people for his name' (Acts 15:14).

God's purpose in the period between the first and second comings of Christ may therefore be expressed as his taking 'a people for his name' out of the world, and in particular out of the Gentile nations. This is referred to by Paul in Romans 11:25 as 'the fullness [or full measure] of the Gentiles'. This was one of the major driving factors in the evangelistic ministry of Paul (cf. Romans 1:13–15; 15:18–20, 24, 28; 1 Corinthians 9:23; 9:16; Colossians 1:25).

The 'fullness of the Gentiles' has its counterpart in the 'fullness of Israel' (cf. Romans 11:17ff.), i.e. that company whom God has determined to bring to himself from among the Jews. These two fullnesses together comprise the church of God, the body of Christ drawn from all the nations and all the ages, 'the fullness of him who fills all in all' (Ephesians 1:23; cf. 2:11–22). God holds back the end until all his people are brought in. This is the force of the word in Matthew 24:14 – the gospel will be preached throughout the whole world, and *then* (i.e. when the fullness from all the nations has been attained) the end will come.

Can we bring back the King?

Does this mean that evangelism on a world-wide basis can be the means of bringing the end in? There is a New Testament reference which may almost say that. In 2 Peter 3:11–12 the apostle refers to the Christian's response to the coming of the end as living lives of 'holiness and godliness, waiting for and *hastening* the coming of the day of God.' The word rendered by 'hastening' is not fully clear and scholars debate its precise meaning. There is, however, much to be said in support of this rendering, used in the RSV main text, and it certainly fits into the teaching to which we have drawn attention.

Is the time of the Lord's coming then in our hands? Such a view was taken by those in an earlier generation who took as their slogan to launch a great campaign for world evangelization: 'Evangelize to a finish and bring back the King' (cf. 2 Samuel 19:10). Put in these terms it would appear to go beyond what Scripture authorizes. Three factors give reason for caution.

(a) We are called to 'bear witness' in all the nations before the end and thus to facilitate the calling out of the Gentiles. But what precisely does this involve? All people hearing the gospel? – surely an almost unthinkable target. A number of Christians among each national group? A number of Christians among each language group? A viable, going church in each nation? All people having the possibility of hearing the gospel even if they do not all avail themselves of it? Since it is not clear what our responsibility precisely is, beyond the general responsibility of witnessing throughout the world, we obviously cannot be certain about the timetable of events which links our evangelism to Christ's return.

(b) The time of the Lord's coming is obviously in the Lord's hands. It is supremely an 'act of God', a sovereign happening in which God acts in his own freedom and lordship to bring history to its close. It will demonstrate, as almost no other event since the creation, the omnipotence and lordship of God over all things. It is therefore surely wrong to see all this as dependent upon the activity of his creatures, as though this mighty act of God hung upon the whims of our human obedience to his command to evangelize.

It is significant that in the passage in 2 Peter 3, which as we have seen possibly comes closest to justifying such a view, Peter has earlier dealt with the reasons for the delay in the Lord's coming (2 Peter 3:1–10), and he does not number the church's failure to fulfil the great commission as one of them. Rather the reason lies in the good pleasure of God himself (verses 9–10) which is tempered by his mercy and forbearance with sinners (verse 9). No doubt our human obedience is one of the factors which God gathers into his act of final salvation, but it is surely wrong to see that act as being determined and controlled by our obedience.

(c) Unless we are very careful this approach to evangelism can become impersonal. We find ourselves preaching the gospel so that men can be saved and the end come. The men being saved then become a means to a greater end. They become no longer ends in themselves but the means to something else. No doubt the coming of the Lord would be for the good of those who are evangelized and come to faith, but still there is just a hint in this approach of people becoming depersonalized, simply numbers to make up the full tally of the elect. But we have only to think of Jesus' own ministry to demolish any idea that leads to impersonalism.

What then may we say about this notion of the 'fullness' of God's people and the end of the age? We need to see that the end is, in some way which we cannot precisely spell out, bound up with the spread of the gospel through the world. We therefore ought to be wholeheartedly committed to evangelism through the world and in every sector of society, in the conviction that evangelism is one of those factors which God makes his instrument in bringing about his final triumph. If this motivation is ever allowed to displace a genuine love and compassion for people, and a deep concern for God's honour and glory as the central motives for evangelism, it is surely mistaken, but as a powerful supplementary motive it surely has its place.

2. Build the church: A second line of action which arises from our conviction of the truth of the Last Things is a concern for the *building up* of the church of Christ world-wide.

One of the great pictures of the church in the New Testament is the bride of Christ (cf. Ephesians 5:21–33; Revelation 21:1ff.). At the Lord's return the church, comprising all the people of God from every age, will be presented to the Lord as a bride is presented to her husband in a wedding service (Revelation 21:2). All God's dealings with his people in the intervening centuries, all his work of renewal and moral transformation, is for the great end that the church might be sanctified and cleansed (Ephesians 5:26) and made fit to be presented perfect to Christ.

There appears clear evidence that Paul saw the church as morally perfected for Christ at his coming (1 Thessalonians 3:13; cf. also 2 Corinthians 11:2; 1 Thessalonians 2:19; 5:23; 3:13; 2 Thessalonians 1:10; Colossians 1:22–23, 28; Jude 24).

Wedding preparations
Scripture also indicates the means by which the church is sanctified and cleansed. Ephesians 4:13 depicts the goal in terms of the church's attaining to 'the measure of the stature of the fullness of Christ', and sees as the means to that end the gifts and ministries of the Holy Spirit in the church: 'apostles ... prophets ... evangelists ... pastors and teachers ... for building up the body of Christ' (4:11, 12). Later he refers to the importance of the word of God (Ephesians 5:26). As God's word is taught among his people, so God sanctifies them. In Colossians 1:28 Paul refers to his own labours to produce this

'mature' Christ-like body as involving preaching, warning and teaching (cf. Acts 20:18–27).

Here then is a great implication of the biblical teaching on the Last Things. The Lord is coming in his glory to call his blood-bought bride to himself. Let us labour and toil to build the church, to sanctify its life, to cleanse it from all that mars and spoils its testimony and its purity, so that when he comes it may be ready for him, 'sound and blameless at the coming of our Lord' (1 Thessalonians 5:23). As we do there is this great encouragement: 'He who calls you is faithful, and he will do it.' (1 Thessalonians 5:24; cf. Jude 24.)

3. Serve our neighbour: The truth of the Last Things also has important implications at the level of involvement in the problems of secular society. There are of course many biblical arguments for the Christian's social involvement and this is far from the only one, but it is one of the most significant.

We have discussed the issues of the millennium (see chapter 6) and have seen that the biblical hope is not purely spiritual. The Bible anticipates a 'new earth' in which righteousness will dwell and in which the various Old Testament pictures of the perfected world will find realization (cf. Psalms 72; 48; Isaiah 2:2–5; 11:1–10; 35:1–10; Micah 4:1–3; Revelation 21–22).

Thus Scripture witnesses to a new coming world in which, even allowing for a real measure of picture and symbol in the biblical language, there will be the realization of all the hopes and dreams of life here and now. In other words there is surely coming a form of perfected human society in a world purged of sin and evil in which the great social values of peace, justice, equality, tolerance, understanding, sympathy, a concern for the vulnerable and the weak, true love for the neighbour, the use of all the resources of the community for the good of the whole, and their like, will find their fulfilment and expression. Conversely all that presently spoils social life and disrupts and embitters human relationships will be banished.

The realization of this dream and these hopes, of course, does not lie on this side of the Lord's coming. But the fact that this perfect society will not appear in history as we know it does not mean that it is irrelevant to history and society. On the contrary it is profoundly relevant in two ways.

The honour of God

First, it gives us in general outline a blueprint for the form of human society which accords with the will of God for man. The perfect human society which lies beyond the Lord's return is therefore the God-ordained goal of human history. It is the form of society which expresses God's perfect will for man, and therefore which honours him and brings eternal glory to his name. This fact establishes the strongest of motives for our working now to try, as far as we may, to bring our present society into conformity with the perfect coming order.

It is equally a supreme motive for struggling to rid our society of all those things which oppose the realization of this order. We use the word 'struggle' advisedly. Obviously the Christian who takes this social obligation seriously is a realist. He will know that unregenerate human nature is poor material with which to work, and he will know that there can be no hopes of establishing Jerusalem on England's green and pleasant land, or anywhere else. The reality will always fall below the ideal, and often so far below as to make the ideal almost incredible. But there will be some hope, even when dealing with fallen men, for God in his common grace and providence holds sin back from having its full head in human life.

The new society is coming

The coming perfect order is relevant in a second and allied sense: the Christian is never driven to final despair even when faced with the appalling intensity and depth of the social problems which confront him. For he knows that every stand he takes for social righteousness and every effort he makes towards social renewal and justice and tolerance is not lost. In his struggle he is moving with the movement of God's purpose. Despite appearances to the contrary the tide is destined to run his way. The ideal society for which he longs will surely come.

True, it will not arise and evolve out of the social process as such, nor will it appear out of social and political revolution as the Marxist imagines. It will come only as God's gift beyond the *parousia*.

It will of course be different in very many respects from society under the conditions of the present age. However, there will be some similarities. Revelation 21:24 says 'the kings of the earth shall bring their glory' into the new Jerusalem. Obviously there is symbol here. Yet this surely says something about the preservation in the new order of all that has been true and righteous and God-honouring in the old. Even if our contribution and struggle appears unavailing at many points in the present, it is not ultimately in vain, but will live on in God's eternal order beyond the end of this age.

These factors combine to represent a significant basis for Christian social concern, for a love of neighbour (which will often mean a love of neighbourhood and society) and therefore for an involvement in society which is a true expression of a Christian belief in the Last Things.

Prayer

If we believe in the Lord's coming and the end of the age then we should pray for it. Jesus set a petition for the coming of the end right at the heart of his pattern for the prayers of his disciples. 'Thy kingdom come!' It is of course true that that prayer received an answer in the ministry of Jesus himself. He brought the kingdom of God in his own person and in his death and resurrection it was established once for all among us (Luke 1:14ff.). But the Lord's Prayer reaches out also to the return of Christ, when the kingdom will fully come. The prayer therefore for those who live 'between the ages' (see chapter 1) becomes a prayer for the return of Christ.

The New Testament expresses this at several other points. It occurs right at the end of the Bible. In Revelation 22:17 'the Spirit and the Bride say "Come."' Here the Holy Spirit is thought of as pleading in unison with the church for the return of the Lord. In verse 20 John almost closes the book (and also the Bible) with the prayer 'Come, Lord Jesus!' In Revelation 6:9–10 the martyrs for Jesus are pictured under the altar in heaven pleading in prayer for the ending of the power of evil in the world and the coming of the end in which God will judge all his enemies.

Nor is this prayer for the Lord's return confined to the last book of Scripture. In 1 Corinthians 16:22 Paul utters the prayer 'Our Lord, Come!' Here then is important evidence in Paul's writings of a habit of prayer for the Lord's coming. In a remarkable passage in Romans 8 Paul refers to the way in which 'the creation', the created order of nature around us, is actually waiting 'with eager longing' (verse 19) for the end and its revelation of God's sons in their glory. If the very stones and hills and skies around us are mutely 'crying out' for the coming glory in which they will all share, how much more ought this to be the heart cry of the sons of God themselves (cf. Titus 2:13)? 2 Peter 3, which speaks of the church on earth as 'hastening' the Lord's coming and the end of the age (3:12), and which we referred to above in the context of evangelism, may also apply to other ways in which the Lord uses his church to draw his purposes in history to their climax. If so, then what more obvious way than by the prayers and intercessions which he inspires within his people.

Watchfulness

One of the clearest indications and implications of the belief in the Last Things according to the New Testament is an attitude of watchfulness. Jesus states this in Matthew 24:42; 25:13; and in the parallel passage in Mark 13 it appears in a number of places (verses 33, 35, 37). Paul makes the same point in 1 Thessalonians 5:4–6. The man or woman who expects the end will be 'sober' and alert. He will not become absorbed in the affairs of this age like the people in Noah's day (Matthew 24:37–39) including perfectly legitimate things like 'eating and drinking, marrying and giving in marriage', so that the Lord's coming will not take him by surprise. All that life brings us in terms of its tender relationships and its fulfilments in work and career and home and so on, important as they are, should never cause us to forget our destiny or lose sight of the future realities and the coming of the Lord. He may not come in our lifetime and we dare not claim that he must, but he certainly may and we are called to be ready.

Love

According to the Lord Jesus the primary characteristic of the disciples of Jesus should be their love for one another (John 13:34–35). The commandment to love one another as he has loved us was his new and special commandment (John 15:12, 17; 1 John 2:7–11; 3:23; 2 John 5–6). There are many reasons for loving one another in the church of God, and one of them flows directly from the fact of the Last Things. For the coming of the Lord and the eternal kingdom means that the relationships which we share in the church are not simply casual and passing attachments. They are everlasting. We will be together in heaven with all the people of God. We are destined for a social, corporate eternity.

This is itself a major argument for love of the brethren. If the prospect of sharing heaven does not make it particularly attractive as far as some of the Lord's people are concerned, we need to take heart from the assurance of Paul that 'we shall all be changed' (1 Corinthians 15:51)! And that includes ourselves as well! When we recognize our common destiny in this way, it helps us to keep in a proper perspective the things which may at the moment cause us to hold back from our brethren. For those people with all their weaknesses and limitations as we now see them (and we have the same no doubt in their eyes!) are destined to be transformed. We are destined to grow from the moral and spiritual pygmies which we may appear at present into the moral giants who will one day reign with Christ in his glory (Revelation 22:4; cf. 1 Corinthians 6:3).

If we are destined for this future glory in the togetherness of the one great and indestructible people of God, then surely we can find it in our hearts to receive them now, and as God pours out his Spirit of love in our hearts (Romans 5:5; Galatians 5:22; 1 Thessalonians 4:9; 1 Corinthians 12:31–13:13) to love them in the love of God's one eternal people.

Joy

When we consider these things – the coming and appearance of the Lord whom we love and who has loved us, the banishing and overthrow of sin and the devil, the establishing of the kingdom of God, the new heaven and earth in which righteousness dwells, the judgement and the righting of earthly wrongs, the destruction of death and sin and disease and pain, and the manifestation of the glory of God – if we truly anticipate them, we are surely possessed at times even in fleeting moments, of a 'joy unspeakable and full of glory' (1 Peter 1:8, Authorized Version).

Obviously part of this joy arises from what all this will mean for us. We shall share his triumph; we shall see the Lord; we shall be delivered from all our personal limitations and the 'sin which clings so closely' (Hebrews 12:1). We shall enter the everlasting kingdom of God with all his people. To contemplate such things is surely to rejoice, and we need not be ashamed of that.

However, our joy will also be for others. When we think of those whom we know or have loved who have experienced acute pain or been subject to bitter disappointment, or carried almost intolerable burdens, or been the victims of terrible ill treatment or laboured under fearful limitations, and then think of their coming fulfilment in Christ and of the fullness of joy which shall then be theirs, we shall surely rejoice in anticipation.

The deepest joy of all, however, should be for what all this will mean to the Lord himself. For on that day he will enter into the inheritance for which he is destined in his universe. All things will be gathered up under Christ (Ephesians 1:22–23), so that at his name 'every knee should bow . . . and every tongue confess that Jesus Christ is Lord' (Philippians 2:10). He will be exalted over all and 'he shall see the fruit of the travail of his soul and be satisfied' (Isaiah 53:11).

Praise

Closely allied to the note of joy in response to God's great coming triumph is that of praise and worship. It is significant in this respect that the heavenly host and the church triumphant, when they are portrayed in the book of Revelation, are depicted as engaged in worship and praise in the light of the coming end (cf. Revelation 5:12ff.; 7:10–12; 11:17–18; 15:3–4; 19:1–5).

The triumph of his grace

The coming triumph of God is simply the carrying into its full realization of the victory, won over sin and death and all the powers of darkness, in the life, death and resurrection of Jesus. It is the bursting into full flower of God's triumph of grace towards his sinful and helpless creatures in Christ. That is why in the vision of the worship of heaven John the seer sees the throne occupied by God and the Lamb and he hears the mighty chorus of the heavenly worship: 'To him who sits upon the throne and to the Lamb be blessing and honour and glory and might for ever and ever!' (Revelation 5:13). Every Christian heart can sound the 'Amen' to this, anticipating the coming triumph of God.

This then is the way in which the Bible's teaching about the Last Things should affect us. Indeed, if they do not, we simply have not grasped the Bible's teaching at all. Christians who truly understand and believe these things will be a people inspired by hope and strengthened in the comfort of God's impending final triumph; they will be earnestly striving to live lives of holiness; they will be committed to action, the spread of the gospel, the growth of the life of the church, the renewal of society; they will be men and women who long and pray and watch for the Lord's appearing, and whose lives are lived in love, joy and praise in expectation of the coming victory.

The help of the Spirit

But where are such people to be found? None of us dare claim that this is his or her portrait. In ourselves we are anything but the sort of person we have just described. There is one other factor, however, to draw into the picture: the Holy Spirit of God. We are not on our own if we belong to the people of God. Our lives are united with God's life by the Holy Spirit. One of the ways the Bible thinks about the Holy Spirit is as we have seen, the life of the new coming age of glory. He is the 'first fruits', the first instalment of that coming new world (Romans 8:23; 2 Corinthians 1:22; 5:5; Ephesians 1:13–14; 4:30). It is his delight to come to our lives, as we open them deliberately to his control, and to bring to reality within us these marks of the life of the future age.

Dawn before daybreak

So, in measure, the miracle takes place and we are enabled to become what in ourselves we are utterly unable to attain to, men and women whose lives accord with the glory of our hope; and as a church to become the people of the hope, a body in whose life the first streaks of the dawn begin to appear with all their promise of that coming daybreak. Then the skies will be torn asunder and the King will appear in his majesty, to be glorified in his saints and to receive the acclaim of his universe. Then all God's enemies will be for ever banished and Christ will reign in his glory, and we will crown him Lord of all to his everlasting honour and praise. Maranatha! Even so, come, Lord Jesus!

FURTHER READING

G. C. Berkouwer, *The Return of Christ* (Eerdmans).
W. J. Grier, *The Momentous Event* (Banner of Truth).
P. E. Hughes, *Interpreting Prophecy* (Eerdmans).
G. T. Manley, *The Return of Jesus Christ* (Inter-Varsity Press).
G. E. Ladd, *The Blessed Hope* (Eerdmans).
I. Murray, *The Puritan Hope* (Banner of Truth).
S. Travis, *The Jesus Hope* (Word).

INDEX

1273